OAKLAND COMMUNITY COLLEGE
MARTIN LUTHER KING, JR.
LEARNING RESOURCES CENTER
27055 ORCHARD LAKE ROAD
FARMINGTON, MICHIGAN 48024

High Wedlock Then Be Honoured

High Wedlock Then Be Honoured

WEDDING POEMS
FROM NINETEEN COUNTRIES AND
TWENTY-FIVE CENTURIES

Edited by Virginia Tufte

 THE VIKING PRESS · NEW YORK

Copyright © 1970 by Virginia James Tufte.
All rights reserved.
First published in 1970 by The Viking Press, Inc.,
625 Madison Avenue, New York, N.Y. 10022.
Published simultaneously in Canada by
The Macmillan Company of Canada Limited.
Library of Congress catalog card number: 69-18806.
Printed in U.S.A.

ACKNOWLEDGMENTS

Martin S. Allwood: Translations of Södergran, "The Land That Is Not," Skjaeraasen, "The Word of God," and Mustapää, "Folk Tale," from *20th Century Scandinavian Poetry*, edited by Martin S. Allwood. Reprinted by permission of Martin S. Allwood.

George Allen & Unwin Ltd.: For seven poems from *The Book of Songs* by Arthur Waley. Published by George Allen & Unwin Ltd. and reprinted by permission.

The Clarendon Press, Oxford: *The Silvae of Statius*, translated by D. A. Slater. Reprinted by permission of the Clarendon Press, Oxford.

Collins-Knowlton-Wing, Inc.: "At the Savoy Chapel" from *Collected Poems 1955* and "The Wedding" from *Love Respelt* by Robert Graves, published by Doubleday & Company. Copyright © 1955 and 1966 by Robert Graves. Reprinted by permission of Collins-Knowlton-Wing, Inc.

J. M. Dent & Sons Ltd.: For "On the Marriage of a Virgin" from *Collected Poems* by Dylan Thomas. Reprinted by permission of J. M. Dent & Sons Ltd. and the Trustees for the copyrights of the late Dylan Thomas.

Estate of Gertrude Stein: For "Prothalamium" by Gertrude Stein. Reprinted by permission of the estate of Gertrude Stein, Daniel C. Joseph, Administrator.

Faber and Faber Ltd.: "Epithalamion" by W. H. Auden from *Collected Shorter Poems 1930–1944*. "Dance Figure" by Ezra Pound from *Personae*. Reprinted by permission of Faber and Faber Ltd.

Harcourt, Brace & World, Inc. and Curtis Brown Ltd.: "Prelude to Space" and "The Small Man Orders His Wedding" from *Poems by C. S. Lewis* edited by Walter Hooper, Copyright © 1964 by the Executives of the Estate of C. S. Lewis. Reprinted by permission of Harcourt, Brace & World, Inc. and Curtis Brown Ltd. "this little bride & groom are" from *Poems 1923–1954* by E. E. Cummings, Copyright 1938 by E. E. Cummings; renewed 1966 by Marion Morehouse Cummings. "Cutting the Jewish Bride's Hair" from *The Marriage Wig and Other Poems* by Ruth Whit-

Acknowledgments

man, Copyright © 1968 by Ruth Whitman. Reprinted by permission of Harcourt, Brace & World, Inc.

Harvard University Press and William Heinemann Ltd.: Verse adaptations based on Maurice Platnauer's prose translation of Claudian, the Loeb Classical Library. Used by permission of Harvard University Press and William Heinemann, Ltd.

H. R. Hays: Translation of "The Ascension and the Assumption" by Ramón López Velarde from *12 Spanish American Poets*. Published by Yale University Press, 1943. Reprinted by permission of H. R. Hays.

David Higham Associates, Ltd.: "Epithalamium" and "Prothalamium" by Dame Edith Sitwell, published by Gerald Duckworth. Reprinted by permission of David Higham Associates, Ltd.

The Hokuseido Press: Translation by R. H. Blyth of nine Senryu from *Senryu*. Reprinted by permission of the Hokuseido Press.

Holt, Rinehart and Winston, Inc. and The Society of Authors: "Epithalamium" from *The Collected Poems of A. E. Housman*. Copyright 1922 by Holt, Rinehart and Winston, Inc. Copyright 1950 by Barclays Bank Ltd. Reprinted by permission of Holt, Rinehart and Winston, Inc. and The Society of Authors. From Ella Isabel Harris's translation of Seneca's *Medea*, which appears in *An Anthology of Roman Drama*, edited by Philip Harsh. Published by Holt, Rinehart and Winston, Inc.

Indiana University Press and Thames and Hudson Ltd.: Samuel Beckett's English translation of *Nox* by Salvador Díaz Miron from *An Anthology of Mexican Poetry* compiled by Octavio Paz. Reprinted by permission of Indiana University Press and Thames and Hudson Ltd.

Alfred A. Knopf, Inc.: For "Upon a Second Marriage." Copyright 1952 by James E. Merrill. Reprinted from *The Country of a Thousand Years of Peace*, by James E. Merrill, by permission of Alfred A. Knopf, Inc.

Macgibbon & Kee Ltd.: "this little bride & groom are" from *Complete Poems* by E. E. Cummings. Reprinted by permission of Macgibbon & Kee Ltd.

The Macmillan Company, King George's Jubilee Trust, and the Society of Authors as the literary representatives of the Estate of John Masefield: For "Prayer for the Royal Marriage" by John Masefield. Reprinted by permission.

Kurt Marti: "*Der ungebetene Hochzeitagast.*" English translation by Christa Wolfe and Virginia Tufte ("The Unbidden Wedding Guest") by permission of the author.

The Marvell Press: "Wedding Wind" by Philip Larkin is reprinted from *The Less Deceived*. Copyright © 1955/1969 by permission of The Marvell Press, 253, Hull Road, Hessle, Yorkshire, England.

New Directions Publishing Corp.: For "On the Marriage of a Virgin" by Dylan Thomas. *Collected Poems*. Copyright 1943 by New Directions Publishing Corporation. "The Marriage" by Yvor Winters, *The Giant Weapon*. Copyright 1943 by New Directions. "Dance Figure" by Ezra Pound from *Personae*. Copyright 1926 by Ezra Pound. All reprinted by permission of New Directions Publishing Corporation.

W. W. Norton & Company Inc. and Russell & Volkening, Inc.: For

Acknowledgments

"Prothalamium" from *Cloud, Stone, Sun, Vine, Poems Selected and New* by May Sarton. Copyright © 1961 by May Sarton. By permission of W. W. Norton & Company, Inc. and Russell & Volkening, Inc.

Oxford University Press: "At the Wedding March" and "Epithalamion" from *The Poems of Gerard Manley Hopkins*, Fourth Edition, ed. W. H. Gardner and N. H. MacKenzie, Copyright © 1967 by Oxford University Press, Inc. Reprinted by permission.

Princeton University Press: "Metal Hoe Hill" and a short quote from page 362 from *Kojiki*, translated with an introduction and notes by Donald Philippi © University of Tokyo Press (1968) co-published by Princeton University Press and University of Tokyo Press. Reprinted by permission of Princeton University Press and Mr. Philippi.

Random House, Inc. "Epithalamion" (*Another Time*) by W. H. Auden. Copyright 1940 and renewed 1968 by W. H. Auden. Reprinted from *The Collected Poetry of W. H. Auden* by permission of Random House, Inc.

The Swallow Press Inc.: Anne Cluysenaar, "Epithalamium," *New Poets of Ireland;* Swallow Press, Chicago: Copyright © 1963 by Donald Carroll.

Vanguard Press, Inc. "Prothalamium" from *Music and Ceremonies* by Edith Sitwell. Copyright © 1959, 1962, 1963 by Dame Edith Sitwell.

The Viking Press, Inc., and Jonathan Cape Ltd.: From *Collected Poems* by James Joyce. Copyright 1918 by B. W. Huebsch, Inc., renewed 1946 by Nora Joyce. Reprinted by permission of The Viking Press, Inc. and Jonathan Cape Ltd.

David Rafael Wang: "The Newlyweds' Cuisine" originally appeared in *Beloit Poetry Journal*, Spring 1959; English translation of Tasso's "To the Father of the Bride"; English translation of a Tahitian lyric and Chinese lyrics. All reprinted by permission of Mr. Wang.

A. P. Watt & Son: "At The Savoy Chapel" from *Collected Poems 1959* (English edition) and "The Wedding" from *Collected Poems 1965* (English edition) by Robert Graves. Reprinted by permission of Robert Graves and A. P. Watt & Son.

Wesleyan University Press: "What We Listened for in Music" by Gray Burr. Copyright © 1969 by Gray Burr. Reprinted from *A Choice of Attitudes* by Gray Burr. "Song for a Marriage" from *Wage War on Silence* by Vassar Miller. Copyright © 1960 by Vassar Miller. Both reprinted by permission of Wesleyan University Press.

Wedding is great Juno's crown:
  O blessed bond of board and bed!
'Tis Hymen peoples every town;
  High wedlock then be honoured.

—WILLIAM SHAKESPEARE

Contents

INTRODUCTION   xxi

Part I: Ancient   1

GREEK

SAPPHO, C. 612 B.C.

    Congratulations: Two Versions   5
    The Bridegroom Is So Tall   5
    To the Bridegroom   6
    The Door-keeper Has Big Feet   6
    Evening Star   6
    To the Bride   7
    Night Singers   7
    Bride's Lament   7

ARISTOPHANES, C. 444–380 B.C.

    Epithalamium from *The Birds:* Take My Wings
      and Dance with Me   8
    Epithalamium from *The Peace:* Midst the Free
      Green Fields   10

EURIPIDES, C. 484–407 B.C.

    From *The Trojan Women:* Cassandra's Epitha-
      lamium   12

THEOCRITUS, C. 316–250 B.C.

    From *Epithalamium for Helen* (Idyll XVIII): Song
      of the Sleepy Bridegroom   15

(ix)

Contents

ROMAN

CATULLUS, C. 84–54 B.C.

Carmen 61: Hymn to Marriage, for Manlius and
    Junia   19
Carmen 62: A Debate on Marriage versus Virginity   27

SENECA, 4 B.C.–A.D. 65

From *Medea:* Epithalamium for Murder   31

STATIUS, C. A.D. 45–96

From *Epithalamium for Stella and Violentilla*
    Why Do You Dally So?   32
    Ah, Now I Know What Day This Is   33
    Of the Night, Let the Bridegroom Sing   35
    Wishes for a Bridal Couple and Their
        Unborn Child   36

MARTIAL, C. A.D. 40–104

For a Son's Marriage   36

AUSONIUS, C. 310–395

To My Wife   37

CLAUDIAN, C. 375–408

From *Epithalamium for Honorius and Maria*
    Palm Tree Mates with Palm   38
    The Hairdresser's Art   39
    Preparing for the Wedding   39
From *Fescennine Verses in Honor of the Marriage
    of the Emperor Honorius*
    Sing, Woods and Rivers All   40
Thorns Arm the Rose   41

ANONYMOUS, 7TH OR 8TH CENTURY

Epithalamium for the Dedication of a Church   42

Contents

ORIENTAL

From the NIHON SHOKI
 Dawn Song (A.D. 513)   44

From the KOJIKI
 Metal Hoe Hill (C. A.D. 450)   45

From THE BOOK OF SONGS, C. 800–600 B.C.
 To the Lady of Ch'i   46
 Companion of Her Lord till Death   47
 Of Silk Is Her Fishing-Line   48
 In the Wicker Fish-Trap   48
 Wind and Rain   49
 Fast Bundled Is the Firewood   49
 Thick Grows the Tarragon   50

Selections from the HAN DYNASTY, 206 B.C.–A.D. 221
 Ancient Quatrain   51
 Marriage Vow   51
 Up the Mountain to Pick Mawu   52

LIU HSI-CHUN, C. 110 B.C.
 Song of Grief   53

From ANCIENT CHINESE *Writing*
 Blues #8   53
 Poems #18   54

TU FU, 712–770
 The Newlyweds' Separation   55

WANG CHIEN, C. 775
 The Newlyweds' Cuisine   56

Contents

CHU CHING-YÜ, BORN 797
    The Toilette   57

Part II: Medieval to Early Renaissance   59

JUDAH HALEVI, 1085?–1140
    To the Choice Bridegroom   63
    Amid the Myrtles   63
    To the Bridegroom   64

JOHN LYDGATE, c. 1370–1451
    From *Epithalamium for Gloucester*   65

WILLIAM DUNBAR, c. 1460–1520
    From *The Thrissil and the Rois*   66

ERASMUS, c. 1466–1536
    Sweet Temper and Mutual Affection   68

ARIOSTO, 1474–1533
    Song for the Third Marriage of Lucrezia Borgia   70

JOHANNES SECUNDUS, 1511–1536
    Epithalamium   75

YU CH'IEN, 1398–1457
    The Honeymooners   81

T'ANG YIN, 1470–1523
    Words for a Picture of Newlyweds   82

Contents

Part III: Renaissance to 1900   83

ENGLISH

SIR PHILIP SIDNEY, 1554–1586
   From *The Countess of Pembroke's Arcadia* (Third Eclogue): O Hymen, Long Their Coupled Joys Maintain!   89

JAMES VI OF SCOTLAND, 1566–1625
   An Epithalamion upon the Marquis of Huntilies Marriage   92

From THE BOOK OF COMMON PRAYER
   Psalm 45, Eructavit cor meum   94

From THE HOLY BIBLE, *Authorized King James Version*
   The Song of Solomon   96

EDMUND SPENSER, 1552–1599
   Epithalamion   102
   Prothalamion   116
   From *The Faerie Queene:* Thames Doth the Medway Wed   122

MICHAEL DRAYTON, 1563–1631
   From *The Muses Elizium:* Prothalamion   127

WILLIAM SHAKESPEARE, 1564–1616
   From *Romeo and Juliet:* Come, Gentle Night   130
   From *As You Like It:* High Wedlock Then Be Honoured   131
   From *A Midsummer Night's Dream:* Blessings on the Bride-Bed   133
   From *The Tempest:* Honour, Riches, Marriage Blessing   135

Contents

WILLIAM SHAKESPEARE *or* JOHN FLETCHER, 1579–1625

   From *The Two Noble Kinsmen:* Roses, Their Sharp Spines Being Gone   137

JOHN DONNE, 1572–1631

   Epithalamion Made at Lincoln's Inn   138
   An Epithalamion, or Marriage Song   141

BEN JONSON, 1573–1637

   From *Masque of Hymen:* Glad Time Is at His Point Arrived   145
   From *Masque of Cupid:* Up, Youths and Virgins, Up, and Praise   149

JOHN WEBSTER, c. 1580–1625

   From *The Duchess of Malfi:* Hark, Now Everything Is Still   152

ROBERT HERRICK, 1591–1674

   An Epithalamie to Sir Thomas Southwell and His Lady   153
   A Nuptial Song, or Epithalamie, on Sir Clipseby Crew and His Lady   159
   Connubii Flores, or the Well-Wishes at Weddings   164
   A Nuptial Verse to Mistress Elizabeth Lee Now Lady Tracy   167
   The Entertainment: or, Porch-verse at the Marriage of Master Henry Northly, and the Most Witty Mistress Lettice Yard   167

JOHN MILTON, 1608–1674

   From *Paradise Lost:* Hail, Wedded Love   168

ANNE BRADSTREET, c. 1612–1672

   To My Dear and Loving Husband   172

Contents

RICHARD CRASHAW, C. 1613–1649

    On Marriage   172
    Epithalamium   172

HENRY VAUGHAN, 1622–1695

    To the Best and Most Accomplished Couple——   177

JOHN DRYDEN, 1631–1700

    From *Amboyna:* Song   179
    From *Marriage-à-la-Mode:* Song   180

ELKANAH SETTLE, 1648–1724

    From *Thalia Triumphans:* A Congratulatory Poem to the Honoured Edmund Morris, Esq., on His Happy Marriage   180

LEON LICHFIELD, C. 1662

    From *Domiduca Oxoniensis:* The Printer, to Her Majesty   182

MATTHEW PRIOR, 1664–1721

    To a Friend on His Nuptials   183

CHRISTOPHER SMART, 1722–1771

    Epithalamium on a Late Happy Marriage   184

WILLIAM BLAKE, 1757–1827

    From *Poetical Sketches:* To the Evening Star   184
    From the Rossetti and Pickering Manuscripts: The Marriage Ring   185
    To My Mirtle   186
    Eternity   186

WILLIAM WORDSWORTH, 1770–1850

    Composed on the Eve of the Marriage of a Friend in the Vale of Grasmere   186

Contents

Percy Bysshe Shelley, 1792–1822
 A Bridal Song   187
 Epithalamium for Charlotte Corday and Francis Ravaillac   188

Anonymous, 1840
 From *The Bride's Marriage-Cake:* Fairy Chorus   190

Alfred Lord Tennyson, 1809–1892
 From *In Memoriam A.H.H.*   192

Gerard Manley Hopkins, 1844–1889
 At the Wedding March   197
 Epithalamion   198

EUROPEAN

Clément Marot, 1496–1544
 Toast to a Departing Duchess   201

Pierre de Ronsard, 1524–1585
 From *Pastoral Song for the Nuptials of Charles, Duke of Lorraine, and Claude, Daughter of the King:* The Wager   202

Gaspar Gil Polo, c. 1530–1591
 From *Diana Enamorada:* Ring Forth, Fair Nymphs, Your Joyful Songs for Gladness   208

Torquato Tasso, 1544–1595
 To the Father of the Bride   211

Pierre Poupo, c. 1552–1591
 Prayers of a Christian Bridegroom   211

(xvi)

Contents

LOPE DE VEGA CARPIO, 1562–1613
    Song for the Divine Bride and Mother   213

GIAMBATTISTA MARINO, 1569–1625
    The Bed   214

From the Circle around SIMON DACH, 1605–1659
    Anke von Tharau   221

JOHANN WOLFGANG VON GOETHE, 1749–1832
    Wedding Song   222

CLEMENS BRENTANO, 1778–1842
    Bridal Song   223

HEINRICH HEINE, 1797–1856
    Knight Olaf   224

CONRAD FERDINAND MEYER, 1825–1898
    Wedding Song   227

ORIENTAL

SEIKI FUJINO, 19TH CENTURY
    Treasure Boat   229

TENRAI KONO, 19TH CENTURY
    Wedding Celebration   230

From collections of SENRYU, 18TH AND 19TH
    CENTURIES   230

Contents

Part IV: Twentieth Century 233

TRANSLATIONS

RUSSIAN FOLK SONGS
   As If from Her Nest 237
   Mariushka's Wedding Song 238

ALEXANDR BLOK, 1880–1921
   I Planted My Bright Paradise 239

BORIS PASTERNAK, 1890–1960
   The Wedding (1957) 240

EINAR SKJÆRAASEN, 1900–
   The Word of God 242

EDITH SÖDERGRAN, 1892–1923
   The Land That Is Not 244

P. MUSTAPÄÄ, 1899–
   Folk Tale 245

KURT MARTI, 1921–
   The Unbidden Wedding Guest 246

RAMÓN LÓPEZ VELARDE, 1888–1921
   The Ascension and the Assumption 247

SALVADOR DÍAZ MIRON, 1859–1928
   Nox 248

ENGLISH

A. E. HOUSMAN, 1859–1936
   Epithalamium 252

(xviii)

Contents

GERTRUDE STEIN, 1874–1946
    Prothalamium for Bobolink and His Louisa A Poem   253

JOHN MASEFIELD, 1878–1967
    Prayer for the Royal Marriage   255

JAMES JOYCE, 1882–1941
    From *Chamber Music*   256

EZRA POUND, 1885–
    Dance Figure   264

EDITH SITWELL, 1887–1964
    Prothalamium   266
    Epithalamium   267

E. E. CUMMINGS, 1894–1962
    this little bride & groom are   268

ROBERT GRAVES, 1895–
    At the Savoy Chapel   269
    The Wedding   270

C. S. LEWIS, 1898–1963
    Prelude to Space   271
    The Small Man Orders His Wedding   272

YVOR WINTERS, 1900–1968
    The Marriage   274

W. H. AUDEN, 1907–
    Epithalamion   275

DYLAN THOMAS, 1914–1953
    On the Marriage of a Virgin   279

Contents

MAY SARTON, 1912–
    Prothalamium   279

GRAY BURR, 1919–
    What We Listened for in Music   281

PHILIP LARKIN, 1922–
    Wedding Wind   281

RUTH WHITMAN, 1923–
    Cutting the Jewish Bride's Hair   282

VASSAR MILLER, 1924–
    Song for a Marriage   283

ANN STANFORD, 1925–
    Ceremonies   284

JAMES MERRILL, 1926–
    Upon a Second Marriage   285

ANNE CLUYSENAAR, 1936–
    Epithalamium   286

GLENN SIEBERT, 1948–
    This and More   288

Introduction

Almost from primitive times, poems have been recited or sung as part of the ritual or celebration of marriage. Folk songs were followed by literary verse, and many of the world's great poets, as well as some lesser ones, wrote poems and songs of this kind. The fashion reached its height in the seventeenth century and waned somewhat in later centuries, but it has never died out. Now, in the closing decades of the twentieth century, there is new interest in wedding poetry. More and more young couples are adding to the wedding ceremony poems or songs of their own choice. Some couples choose favorite passages from traditional literature, others choose contemporary readings. Now and then a bridegroom and bride, or their friends, compose verse or prose of their own to be sung or read.

I became interested in the tradition of nuptial poetry about ten years ago, and I found that through the ages, literally thousands of poems of this kind have been written by both established writers and amateurs. I discovered also that few collections of such poems have ever been made, and none has been published in the twentieth century. From the several hundred that I collected I have chosen something over a hundred; eighteen countries are represented, and about twenty-five centuries. Most of the poems are from the western world, about half of them from England and the United States. I have included a somewhat random sampling from the Orient.

I have tried to choose poems to illustrate the wide distribution and variety of this single form of poetry in both time and space. Even though this book is probably the largest collection of nuptial verse ever published, it is still not a comprehensive anthology of major poems from every country, or indeed from any one country, but a somewhat arbitrary collection of poems that I hope modern readers will enjoy.

The arrangement of the poems is chronological: Ancient, Medi-

Introduction

eval to Early Renaissance, Renaissance to 1900, and Twentieth Century. Within each part, there are more or less geographical groups.

In general, the poetry speaks for itself, but I have written notes for some of the poems, describing special circumstances, customs, or occasions. In a few instances where extracts appear rather than complete poems, I have tried to summarize the omitted context. The general introduction, and the introductions to the book's four parts, are intended to highlight the continuity of this form of poetry—a form with a recorded history of three thousand years.

Throughout the world, nuptial poetry has developed, I think, as one aspect of the social recognition which characterizes marriage as an institution. The wedding ceremony itself signifies not only the couple's desire to assume the privileges and duties of marriage, but also society's recognition of marriage as an institution, and society's sanction of the particular union. The poet may be speaking simply as a friend or relative, but more often he is, in a way, speaking on behalf of the social establishment as he praises the institution of marriage, congratulates the couple, and describes the events of the wedding day. On occasion, however, the poet's voice is a dissident one, and he employs the devices of the nuptial poem ironically, sometimes censuring society and its institutions rather than praising them. I have included in this collection a few dissident and other "dark" nuptial poems, as well as two other variants—poems having to do with mystical marriage and with union in nature.

In Europe, wedding poems have from classical times been called *epithalamia*, a Greek word that means *at the couch* or *nuptial chamber*, and probably in its early use referred to folk songs, perhaps shouted or sung by friends of the couple in the street or at the bedroom door just before consummation of the union. Songs of this kind are mentioned by Homer in the *Iliad*, as he describes the wedding scene on the shield of Achilles, a scene in which the young men and women exchange songs as they dance through the streets in a bridal procession, while the older matrons stand in their doors and watch approvingly. Sappho's wedding songs, of which we have only fragments, were composed in the seventh century before Christ, possibly to celebrate the marriages of young women who were her students. Also dating back many centuries is the Biblical Song of Songs, some-

Introduction

times called a sacred epithalamium, probably composed as a celebration of human marriage, later allegorized by the Church fathers as relating to the union of Christ and the Church.

In England, wedding songs had their greatest popularity during Shakespeare's time, and just afterward, and it is one of Shakespeare's nuptial songs that gives this book its title, *High Wedlock Then Be Honoured*. The masterpiece in all of English nuptial poetry was written by Shakespeare's contemporary, Edmund Spenser, to celebrate his own wedding in 1594.

Many of the poems in this book were written for kings, queens, and other members of royal families—for the wedding of James IV of Scotland and Princess Margaret Tudor in 1503, of Charles I of England and Henrietta Maria in 1625, of Queen Victoria and Prince Albert in 1840, and of Queen Elizabeth II and Prince Philip in 1947. And one royal author has been included, the young James VI of Scotland, later to become James I of England, who wrote a wedding masque for a friend. An author of more humble station was the printer who in 1662 set the type for about a hundred nuptial poems written by Oxford University students for Charles II and his bride, Katherine of Portugal. When the printer had finished setting the students' poems into type, he wrote a poem of his own and printed it on the last page of the book.

Most of the poems here were not written by amateurs, however, but by poets of considerable reputation, many of them known for their plays or epics as well as for lyrics. Several classical poets—Sappho, Aristophanes, Euripides, Theocritus, and especially Catullus—left a great heritage. Catullus's Carmen 61 and Spenser's *Epithalamion* (reproduced here in their entirety) have served as models for hundreds of other works, especially during the Renaissance, an era when almost every English poet tried his hand at writing nuptial songs. John Donne, Ben Jonson, and John Milton are among those represented here. Although many of these English poets drew inspiration from the classical and later Latin authors, others took Italian wedding poems as their models, drawing on Tasso's sonnets or Marino's erotic narrative epithalamia. Still others borrowed from the intricate pastoral epithalamia devised by French poets of the Pléiade, especially Ronsard and Belleau.

Marriage rites in many societies include the groom's mock cap-

Introduction

ture of the bride and the accompanying battle and victory. Walter Starkie (in *UCLAN Review*, Spring 1963) describes ancient nuptial rites as practiced by the gypsies, descendants of the band from Greece that in 1417 spread through western Europe. He tells how an old woman, who in the ceremony is called the *picaora*, entered the bridal apartment after the consummation and displayed to the guests evidence that the bride had been a virgin, whereupon the gypsy song of virginity was sung. In other societies also, it was customary for the attendants to exhibit ceremonially the coverlet from the nuptial bed as evidence of the struggle and victory.

In every era and country, one of the main topics of the wedding poem was the bride's beauty. Although the conventional European heroine of lyric poetry was blond, with "hair like golden wire," poets were often called upon to celebrate the beauty of a brown-haired girl. Marot solved the problem by solemnly declaring of the Princess Magdalaine, daughter of the King of France, "She is brunette, *but* she is beautiful." Usually the poet went on to assert that the bride's beauty was only a reflection of her inward goodness and purity. And poets always paid conventional tribute to the bride's virginity. The Italian poet Ariosto, in his Latin epithalamium honoring the third marriage of Lucrezia Borgia, described the bride as "a beautiful virgin."

Some of the most glowing tributes in English were written in 1613 for a bride who was later charged with plotting the most notorious murder of the seventeenth century. When the Lady Frances Howard and the Earl of Somerset were married, John Donne, George Chapman, and many others wrote wedding poems for them. Not long afterward, the couple was charged, along with four accomplices, with poisoning Sir Thomas Overbury, poet and essayist. Ironically, Overbury's most famous work was a poem called "The Wife," which pictured the virtues a young man should expect to find in a woman.

In many wedding poems, the poet described the virtues of both bride and bridegroom and often, as well, indulged in praise of the ancestry, achievements, learning, and wealth of their parents and other relatives. The kind of tribute to be paid to the two families received the attention of Greek and Roman teachers of rhetoric, who set forth rules and topics for writers of wedding poems and orations. Young poets were advised to give equal space to the families of bride and groom, and a number of poets followed this advice to the letter, giving precisely the same number of lines or stanzas to the two families.

Wedding poets followed other advice from these classical teachers, and also the advice of the sixteenth-century Italian critic Scaliger. He, and others, recommended comparisons of the couple to aspects of nature, and so there have been hundreds of brides compared to fruit and flowers, and bridegrooms to trees. The favorite comparison involved the ivy and the oak, or the vine and the elm—the wife being the vine clinging to and supported by the sturdy tree.

Wedding poets were advised to praise not only the couple and their families but also the marriage gods—Hymen, Jupiter, and Juno—and to invoke repeatedly the principal deity, Hymen, god of generation. Thus came into being the hymeneal refrain, which continued in many poems long after pagan deities gave way to Christian. At various times, wedding poets were advised to describe heavenly blessings, pagan or Christian, along with the more immediate earthly benefits—social, financial, and personal—to be derived from legal marriage. Poets were urged to stress the importance of the family as an institution and to include a prayer or wish for offspring. Thus it was essential for the poet to urge the couple to unite in love, and for the poet to assert strongly that such union was in accord with nature, inasmuch as the process of generation and conception was common to plants, animals, and all of nature. In this connection, Scaliger and other writers also advised wedding poets to exercise modesty, although they might indulge in gentle jesting.

Traditionally, epithalamia include what is called a *fescennine* passage—usually a bit of ribald humor directed at the bridegroom. A superstition underlies this custom, the idea that man is most vulnerable when he thinks himself most fortunate, and that evil spirits will get him unless he is taken down by scurrilous remarks or teasing. Although this excuse is given for bawdiness, there is a built-in restraint in that wedding poems are almost always public poems. But the subject matter itself, of course, makes *double-entendre* almost inevitable.

As the voice of society, the epithalamium tends to be didactic rather than frivolous, and to be both personal and universal. It is at times a form of marriage counsel, especially for young brides—and many brides of earlier centuries were only twelve or thirteen years

Introduction

old. Often the poet addresses the bride directly with words intended to allay her fears and to instruct her on her responsibilities. Catullus advises the young bride not to deny her husband those favors proper to marriage, lest he go elsewhere to find them. The same poet advises the bridegroom to put off the habits of bachelorhood that are not appropriate to a husband. Many poets warn the couple about typical problems of marriage—"lawless lust," jealousy, churlish words, and slovenly housekeeping. Poets urge the couple to work out their problems, to resolve disruptive elements, and to strive for harmony and peace.

The marital union is often portrayed as a microcosm, becoming a metaphor expressing the poet's desire for universal harmony and peace. To relate human marriage to the cosmos is a typical Renaissance practice, and it is often accompanied by the ancient theme of the unions of rivers and other forces of nature. But marriage as microcosm is not limited to Renaissance poetry. It is a frequent theme in nuptial poems of the twentieth century, especially those written in wartime, among them poems by Gertrude Stein, A. E. Housman, W. H. Auden, and Robert Graves.

From very early times nuptial poetry has had several motives other than the celebration of human marriage. During the Middle Ages the epithalamium celebrated "high wedlock" in a special sense, when the *Song of Solomon* and Psalm 44 of the Vulgate were interpreted by churchmen as celebrations of mystical marriages—Christ and the Church, Christ and the Virgin Mary, or Christ and the human soul. Conventions of the classical nuptial poem were employed in hundreds of Latin hymns called epithalamia, written as tributes to the Virgin Mary or to various saints, or to celebrate occasions such as the birth of a child, the dedication of a church, or the taking of vows by a nun. Thus in the Middle Ages the same sort of poem might be a tribute to marriage or to virginity. Even in the twentieth century a few poets have written sacred nuptial poems, poems celebrating mystical unions.

Many of these epithalamia utilized themes from both pagan and Christian nuptial poetry. Christ, the Virgin Mary, and the angels sometimes appear in the same poem as the classical Venus, Juno, and Cupids. Or the chariot of Venus drawn by swans or doves is taken over by Christ, and the heathen attendants are replaced by *Pax, Pudor,*

Introduction

and *Pietas*. A chariot like that of Venus accommodates brides of the Church, or the Evangelists, or even becomes the chariot of the Church. Instead of Love animating Chaos as in the pagan mythology, it is God himself who sanctions marriage by creating Eve. In some of the medieval poems, Christ replaces Hymen as speaker and serves as *pronuba* in the bridal chamber, adorning the maiden with virtues.

In addition to human and mystical unions, nuptial poems through the ages have dealt with various kinds of unions in nature. Greek and Roman rhetoricians urged the wedding poet to compare marriage of human beings to unions of various elements of nature. Along with unions of flowers and trees, European poets portrayed unions of rivers, and of creatures living in the water—dolphins, whales, fish, the swans of Venus, the swans on the Thames or the Po. The association of rivers, streams, springs—and of water and its cosmic generative function—with the institution of human marriage was by Spenser's time a long-established convention. Sometimes one union of streams represented the union of two royal houses.

In the nuptial poem for human beings, the bride and bridegroom take on the attributes of rivers. In the nature nuptial poem, or topographical epithalamium, the comparison is reversed: the union of two rivers is compared to the marriage of human beings, and the rivers assume the attributes of man and woman, the bride, in particular, being described like a human bride, as in Spenser's poem for the union of the rivers Thames and Medway.

Renaissance poets often regarded writing nuptial poetry as a kind of game, and displayed their ingenuity by employing such devices as acrostics in which the first and last letters of the poem's lines spell out the names of the couple; some of them wrote poems called *centos*, composed entirely of a patchwork of lines or half-lines from Virgil or other selected poets. And some of them wrote poems shaped like altars or eggs or other objects. The union of rivers or other aspects of nature was not usually this sort of game, however, but a device leading to a somewhat melancholy reflection: Union is only temporary. Although it brings regeneration, the union itself ends in dispersion and death. Indeed, very early in the tradition, nuptial folk songs and nature poems may have been associated with fertility rituals and dramas of generation and death, out of which the great modes of comedy and tragedy probably developed.

Introduction

From two early Greek comedies, Aristophanes' *The Birds* and *The Peace*, Ann Stanford has translated for this book two nuptial songs—the first an imitation of the extravagant praise customary for wealthy town couples, and the second a rustic poem with characteristic country humor. Through the centuries, nuptial poems and songs have continued to be associated with comedy. Robert Burton remarked in the seventeenth century that it was customary to conclude a comedy with a wedding and shaking of hands. And he might have added that it was also customary to include a wedding song. Shakespeare's *As You Like It* and *A Midsummer Night's Dream* are examples.

A quite different sort of bridal song in drama—the tragic or ironic one—may have given rise to the dark nuptial poems I have mentioned earlier. From Euripides' tragedy *The Trojan Women*, Miss Stanford has translated the sad nuptial song of Cassandra, who as a captive of war must become the bride of the enemy's leader, Agamemnon. Cassandra promises that through this marriage she will bring the enemy's destruction and her people's revenge. Her song is one of a type often seen in tragedy, a song that appears in conjunction with an improper or unsanctioned union. Usually the song presages murder or other untimely death, revenge, war, or other disaster. Additional examples from tragedies may be seen in Seneca's *Medea*, Webster's *The Duchess of Malfi*, and Shakespeare's *Romeo and Juliet*.

Other dark or ironic uses of the nuptial theme appear in Samuel Beckett's translation of "Nox" by the Mexican poet Salvador Díaz Miron, in C. S. Lewis's "Prelude to Space, An Epithalamium," and in Edith Sitwell's "Epithalamium." The darkness, disunion, and disorder portrayed in these variants help to point up the essential quality of the normal wedding poem: it is basically a celebration of union, enacting a pattern of order.

Although the poems in this book are diverse, the reader will find many similarities between poems widely separated in space and in time. As a rather general symbol of fertility and hope for the future, the fish is seen in poems from both the western world and the Orient. Birds of several kinds represent love and conjugal devotion—turtledoves and swans in the European poems, mandarin ducks in the Japanese and Chinese lyrics. Flowers have long been part of the alphabet of love and marriage in every country.

Introduction

Everywhere, nuptial poetry carries out the dual role of poetry in general, as described by the poet Horace—to delight and to teach. Ben Jonson's words about poetry seem to apply especially to nuptial verse: "It . . . offers to mankind a certain rule and pattern of living well and happily, disposing us to all civil offices of society."

The nuptial poet has honored and perhaps helped to perpetuate one of society's most durable but ever-changing institutions. The role of women has changed through the centuries, and the role of men as well, and the institution of marriage has gradually adapted to these changes. Young men and women today have many choices that were unavailable in even the recent past, but they continue to love, to unite, to have children, and to seek comfort and companionship in each other. Poets will no doubt continue to write about these experiences, as they have for three thousand years, and to view the marriage commitment as an expression of faith and hope.

NOTE: *All translations not otherwise credited are by the editor.*

PART I

Ancient

E̶CHOES OF FOLK SONGS may be heard in the three groups of our earliest written nuptial poetry—Greek, Roman, and Oriental.

From ancient Greece, the earliest extant nuptial songs are those of Sappho, probably written near the end of the seventh century B.C. and later collected into a book by her Alexandrian editors. Of these, only brief fragments survive.

Aristophanes, in the nuptial songs that conclude two of his bawdy comedies, *The Birds* and *The Peace,* may have been imitating Sappho's poems or parodying those of her successors who had indulged in extravagant praise of the bridal couple. Though playful and exaggerated, both songs celebrate marriages that symbolize the hope for unity and peace in the nation. The rustic humor in *The Peace* calls to mind the fertility rites which may have preceded the development of Greek drama.

Euripides' tragic nuptial song from *The Trojan Women* portrays the miseries of war. The pastoral wedding song of Theocritus concerns Helen of Troy and Menelaus, and is sung by twelve noble Spartan virgins, who jest prettily with the bridegroom.

The Roman section is headed by Catullus, the most important nuptial poet in the classical tradition. In his Carmen 61, the hymn for the marriage of Manlius and Junia, the poet assumes the role of master of ceremonies, directing the events of the wedding day and commenting on them. His Carmen 62 is a singing contest between a chorus of young men and a chorus of virgins, friends of the bridal couple. Perhaps the classical singing match is the inspiration for the modern fraternity-sorority singing matches, still held in some American universities when couples announce their engagements. A stark contrast in mood comes with the darkness and horror of Seneca's *Medea,* in

Part I: Ancient

which a nuptial song for Jason and his new bride is paralleled by the lines spoken by Medea, Jason's former wife, as she plots revenge and murder.

One of the first of many long narrative nuptial poems, sometimes called rhetorical or epic epithalamia, is that of Statius, written about A.D. 90 for a bridegroom named Stella and his bride Violentilla. It is much too long to be included in its entirety, but four extracts are given, one of them arguing for the doctrine of increase often heard in nuptial poetry, the idea that marital union is in accord with nature. Birds and flocks and savage beasts unite. Should man do less? The sky itself weds earth, and thus it is that life renews itself, all things after their own kind.

Brief songs by Martial and Ausonius are concerned with the companionship which marriage brings as a couple grows old. Ausonius also wrote a long and notorious nuptial cento—a patchwork of lines from Virgil—not included here. Ausonius himself admitted that he blushed twice over for converting Virgil's words to immodest discussion of secrets of bedchamber and couch, but he justified such freedom because the public liked it, he said, and also *fescennine* bawdry protected the couple from the evil eye.

Fescennine verses by Claudian are included in this section, verses written to accompany his 341-line epic on the marriage of the Emperor Honorius and Maria. Extracts from the epic are included here, one of them a passage in which the goddess Venus, dressing her hair, carefully leaves untouched a straying tress because such seeming disarray is seductive. The last poem in the Roman section is a sacred epithalamium, a hymn written for the dedication of a church.

Dates of many of the Oriental songs are unknown, but some of those appearing here may be earlier than the songs of Sappho. The dates of those from the *Book of Songs* may range from 800 to 600 B.C. The Japanese lyrics, and some of the Chinese, are from later centuries.

Greek

SAPPHO, c. 612 B.C.

Congratulations: Two Versions

Fortunate bridegroom,
the match you prayed for is made,
and the mate you prayed for is yours.
Your bride is most comely,
her eyes honey-sweet,
her beauty alight with Love's smile.
Aphrodite has blessed you indeed.

You lucky man, you.
Here you are married, as you wanted to be,
And you have the girl you wanted.
She's such a pretty girl, too,
And she loves you.
You can see it in her eyes,
And her smile,
And the way her face shines.
Love has been good to you.

The Bridegroom Is So Tall

Lift high the roof beams, carpenters!
Praise Hymen!
The bridegroom towers god-like,
Praise Hymen!

Part I: Ancient

Taller than the tallest man,
He surpasses all, as the poets of Lesbos
Surpass the poets of other lands.

To the Bridegroom

A bowl full of ambrosia
   now has been mixed,
   and Hermes takes the wine-jug
   and pours for the gods.

Then all drain the wine-cups
   and make ritual libation,
   portending for the bridegroom
   all things that are good.

The Door-keeper Has Big Feet

THE DOOR-KEEPER who guarded the bridal chamber to keep out the couple's friends and relatives was sometimes the target of jests.

The door-keeper's feet are seven fathoms long.
Five bulls' hides it takes
And ten shoemakers to make
A pair of sandals to fit him.

Evening Star

Evening Star, you bring together
All things that daytime divides.
You bring the sheep,
You bring the goats.
And the children to their homes
(And men to the arms of their brides.)

SAPPHO

To the Bride

Bride, so filled with rosy longings,
Bride, fair ornament of Love's queen,
Come now to nuptial couch,
Come now to bed, to sweet and gentle sport,
To your bridegroom, come.

Full willing,
You shall find the path
With evening star as guide
To Matrimony's silver throne
And wedlock's wonder.

Night Singers

May the bridesmaids
all night long
sing of the love
of you and your bride,
adorned with violets.

Bride's Lament

BRIDE

Maidenhood,   maidenhood,
where have you gone?

MAIDENHOOD

I have gone forever.
Forever.

Part I: Ancient

ARISTOPHANES, c. 444-380 B.C.
Translated by Ann Stanford

Take My Wings and Dance with Me
Epithalamium from *The Birds*

MESSENGER

O all-happy, successful, O too great for words!
O winged race of birds, thrice blessed!
Welcome your king back to your fortunate dwellings.
For he is drawing near, and neither the all-bright star
Shedding its beams from the gold-gleaming heaven
Nor the blaze of the far-flashing rays of the sun
Shine with more glaring splendor. He is coming!
Bringing a wife, her beauty inexpressible,
Wielding the thunderbolt, the winged shaft of Zeus.
An indescribable perfume rises to the sky
Coils of smoke drifting before the easy wind
And scattering far and wide. What a spectacle!
And he is here! Now let us commence to sing
Songs of the Muse, sacred, of favoring omen.

CHORUS

Lead on, divide, lead aside, get away!
Fly around
This happy man of happy fortune.
O what manhood! O what beauty!
Marriage most blessed for our state!

Great, great is the good fortune
The race of birds
Possesses through this man.

ARISTOPHANES

With wedding songs and bridal odes
Greet him and his Basilea.

With such a wedding song
Moira, goddess of Fate
Brought Olympian Hera
To the bed of Zeus
Lord of the lofty thrones.
Hymen, O Hymenaeus, O!

And Eros, blooming
And golden-winged
Stretched back the reins,
The charioteer for the wedding
Of Zeus and the happy Hera.
Hymen, O Hymenaeus, O!
Hymen, O Hymenaeus, O!

PITHETAERUS

I am pleased with your songs, I am pleased with
    your odes. I admire your words

CHORUS

Come now and celebrate
His thunder that shakes the earth
The mighty fire of his lightning
And his terrible bright thunderbolt.

O great golden streak of lightning!
O mighty, immortal shaft, bearing fire!
O earth-cracking thunders that bring the rain
With which this man now shakes the earth!
Like a god he holds sway over all
For he holds Basilea, the assistant of Zeus.
Hymen, O Hymenaeus, O!

Part I: Ancient

PITHETAERUS

Now let all the wing-borne race
Follow the bridal pair
Up to the floor of Zeus
And the marriage bed.
And now, my dear, stretch out your hands
And take my wings and dance with me.
I am going to lift you up
And carry you through the air.

CHORUS

Io Paean! Alalalae!
Hail, glorious victory!
O highest of the gods!

Midst the Free Green Fields
Epithalamium from *The Peace*

CHORUS

It is time to say words of good omen and for some to bring forth the bride
And for us to take torches and everyone dance and rejoice.
We can take all the farming tools back to the fields
After we've danced and poured wine and chased out Hyperbolus.
And after we pray to the gods
To give riches to the Hellenes
And to grant us a good crop of barley
And that we have plenty of wine
And munch figs
And that our wives bring forth for us
And that all the good things that we lost
Be brought together as they were before
And that the fiery sword be put away.

ARISTOPHANES

TRYGAEUS

Come here, wife, to the fields
And pretty as you are
Lie down prettily with me.
Hymen, Hymenaeus, O!
Hymen, Hymenaeus, O!

CHORUS

Thrice happy man!
It is right that good fortune
Pours out upon you!
Hymen, Hymenaeus, O!
Hymen, Hymenaeus, O!

FIRST SEMI-CHORUS

What shall we do with her?
What shall we do with her?

SECOND SEMI-CHORUS

We'll gather ripe fruit from her!
We'll gather ripe fruit from her!

FIRST SEMI-CHORUS

Let the rest of us
Whose task it is
Hoist up the groom and carry him.
Hymen, Hymenaeus, O!
Hymen, Hymenaeus, O!

SECOND SEMI-CHORUS

And may you live happily,
Without troubles, and freely
All the time gathering figs.

Part I: Ancient

Hymen, Hymenaeus, O!
Hymen, Hymenaeus, O!

FIRST SEMI-CHORUS

His large and thick.

SECOND SEMI-CHORUS

But hers is sweet!

TRYGAEUS

So you will say
All the while you eat
And the good wine flows.

CHORUS

Hymen, Hymenaeus, Io!
Hymen, Hymenaeus, Io!

TRYGAEUS

Here's to you, gentlemen!
If you come with me
You'll have still more cakes.

* * *

EURIPIDES, c. 484-407 B.C.
Translated by Ann Stanford

Cassandra's Epithalamium
From *The Trojan Women*

WHEN TROY was taken by the Greeks, the princesses of the House of Priam were apportioned by lot to the leaders of the victorious army.

EURIPIDES

Polyxena was assigned to be the bride of Achilles' ghost, an event later noted in the nuptial song of Catullus's Carmen 64. Hecuba was allotted to Odysseus; Andromache to the son of Achilles; and Cassandra, daughter of Hecuba and Priam, was assigned to be the concubine of King Agamemnon. With prophetic knowledge of the tragic events to come, Cassandra in the white robes and wreaths of a priestess sings her own epithalamium, waving a blazing torch and dancing wildly.

> Hold it up, show it, bring the torch!
> I worship with flame.
> Look! look!
> I light up this holy place!
> Hymen, Hymenaeus, Lord
> Blessed the bridegroom
> Blessed I too
> Whose wedding song leads to the bed
> Of a king in Argos.
>
> Seeing that you, mother, can only weep
> And lament for the death of my father
> And cry out over our loved country,
> I must light the fire of the torch
> For my own wedding.
> *To the brightness! to the glory!*
> I offer to you, O wedding god.
> And you, O Hecate, give light
> For the marriage bed of a maid, as is the custom.
>
> Whirl, feet high in the air.
> Lead on the chorus.
> *Evan! Evoi!*
> As when my father's fortune
> Was most blessed.
> Apollo—thou—
> Lead the ritual chorus.

Part I: Ancient

I perform your rites
In your temple among the laurels.

Dance, mother, lead on,
Turn your feet here and there with mine
Carry the sweet steps.
Call out the *Hymen, O*
In happy song
And the shout for the bride.
Come, maidens of Phrygia,
Splendidly dressed
Sing for my wedding
And for the husband
Fate sends to lie beside me.

Mother, crown me with wreaths of victory.
And be glad for this my marriage to a king.
Escort me, and if I seem to you unwilling
Push me away with force. If Apollo lives still
Helen's marriage was not so troublesome
As mine will be to the great Agamemnon.

Mother, there is no need to pity this your land
Nor weep over my marriage. For by this joining
I shall destroy those that both of us hate the most.
Go now, quickly, that I may quickly wed the
    bridegroom in the house of death.
O, leader of the Greeks with your haughty vision of
    great deeds—
Evil man, you will be vilely buried, by night, not
    in the light of day.
And I—my dead body will be thrown into a gully, naked
Into streams filled by winter rains, close by the grave of
    the bridegroom

Given to wild beasts to tear to pieces—the servant of Apollo!
I am done with the temple-feasts which were my joy
    in other days.
Garlands of the god most loved by me, holy ornaments,
    farewell.
See! I tear them from my body while it is still my own
    and chaste
And give them to the winds to carry to you, lord of oracles.

Where is the ship of the general? Where must I go to embark?
No longer will you be the first to watch for the wind in the sails
Who take me away from this land—one of the three
    Avengers.
Say goodbye to me, mother, do not cry. Loved place
    where I was born
And brothers down there in the earth and father who begot us
Soon you will welcome me. But I shall come to death
    victorious
Having destroyed the House of Atreus which has ruined
    us utterly.

* * *

THEOCRITUS, c. 316-250 B.C.
Translated by John Dryden

Song of the Sleepy Bridegroom
From *Epithalamium for Helen* (Idyll xviii)

THEOCRITUS'S HUMOR is more subtle than Sappho's taunts at the big-footed doorkeeper and Aristophanes' rustic bawdry. In this wedding song for Helen and Menelaus, a chorus of the bride's friends teases

Part I: Ancient

the bridegroom on the wedding night, asking why he wants to go to bed so early and suggesting that he's sleepy because he's had too much wine.

>Twelve Spartan virgins, noble, young, and fair,
>With violet wreaths adorned their flowing hair;
>And to the pompous palace did resort,
>Where Menelaus kept his royal court.
>There, hand in hand, a comely choir they led,
>To sing a blessing to his nuptial bed,
>With curious needles wrought, and painted flowers be-
>   spread.
>Jove's beauteous daughter now his bride must be,
>And Jove himself was less a god than he;
>For this their artful hands instruct the lute to sound,
>Their feet assist their hands, and justly beat the ground.
>This was their song:—Why, happy bridegroom, why,
>Ere yet the stars are kindled in the sky,
>Ere twilight shades, or evening dews are shed,
>Why dost thou steal so soon away to bed?
>Has Somnus brushed thy eyelids with his rod,
>Or do thy legs refuse to bear their load,
>With flowing bowls of a more generous god?
>If gentle slumber on thy temples creep,
>(But, naughty man, thou dost not mean to sleep,)
>Betake thee to thy bed, thou drowsy drone,
>Sleep by thyself, and leave thy bride alone:
>Go, leave her with her maiden mates to play
>At sports more harmless till the break of day;
>Give us this evening; thou hast morn and night,
>And all the year before thee, for delight.
>O happy youth! to thee, among the crowd
>Of rival princes, Cupid sneezed aloud;
>And every lucky omen sent before,
>To meet thee landing on the Spartan shore.

THEOCRITUS

Of all our heroes, thou canst boast alone,
That Jove, whene'er he thunders, calls thee son.
Betwixt two sheets thou shalt enjoy her bare,
With whom no Grecian virgin can compare;
So soft, so sweet, so balmy, and so fair.
A boy, like thee, would make a kingly line;
But oh! a girl like her must be divine.
Her equals we in years, but not in face,
Twelve score viragos of the Spartan race,
While naked to Eurotas' banks we bend,
And there in manly exercise contend,
When she appears are all eclipsed and lost,
And hide the beauties that we made our boast.

So, when the night and winter disappear,
The purple morning, rising with the year,
Salutes the spring, as her celestial eyes
Adorn the world and brighten all the skies;
So beauteous Helen shines among the rest,
Tall, slender, straight, with all the Graces blest.
As pines the mountains, or as fields the corn,
Or as Thessalian steeds the race adorn;
So rosy coloured Helen is the pride
Of Lacedaemon, and of Greece beside.
Like her no nymph can willing osiers bend
In basket-works, which painted streaks commend;
With Pallas in the loom she may contend.
But none, ah! none can animate the lyre,
And the mute strings with vocal souls inspire;
Whether the learned Minerva be her theme,
Or chaste Diana bathing in the stream,
None can record their heavenly praise so well
As Helen, in whose eyes ten thousand Cupids dwell.
O fair, O graceful! yet with maids enrolled,
But whom tomorrow's sun a matron shall behold!

Part I: Ancient

Yet ere tomorrow's sun shall show his head,
The dewy paths of meadows we will tread,
For crowns and chaplets to adorn thy head.
Where all shall weep, and wish for thy return,
As bleating lambs their absent mother mourn.
Our noblest maids shall to thy name bequeath
The boughs of Lotos, formed into a wreath.
This monument, thy maiden beauty's due,
High on a plane-tree shall be hung to view;
On the smooth rind the passenger shall see
Thy name engraved, and worship Helen's tree;
Balm, from a silver box, distilled around,
Shall all bedew the roots, and scent the sacred ground.
The balm, 'tis true, can aged plants prolong,
But Helen's name shall keep it ever young.
Hail bride, hail bridegroom, son-in-law to Jove!
With fruitful joys Latona bless your love!

Let Venus furnish you with full desires,
Add vigour to your wills, and fuel to your fires!
Almighty Jove augment your wealthy store,
Give much to you, and to his grandsons more!
From generous loins a generous race will spring,
Each girl, like you, a queen; each boy, like you, a king.
Now sleep, if sleep you can; but while you rest,
Sleep close, with folded arms, and breast to breast.
Rise in the morn; but oh! before you rise,
Forget not to perform your morning sacrifice.
We will be with you ere the crowing cock
Salutes the light, and struts before his feathered flock.
Hymen, Oh Hymen, to thy triumphs run,
And view the mighty spoils thou hast in battle won!

Roman

CATULLUS, c. 84-54 B.C.

Hymn to Marriage, for Manlius and Junia
Carmen 61

Oh, you who live on the Heliconian mountain,
Child of Urania,
You who capture the tender girl for the man,
Oh Hymenaeus Hymen
Oh Hymen Hymenaeus

Wreathe your head with blossoms
Of sweet-scented marjoram,
Put on the flame-colored marriage veil,
Come, Hymen, joyfully come,
Wearing on snow-white foot the yellow slipper

And roused by the joyful day,
Singing nuptial songs with ringing voice,
Beat the earth with your feet,
With your hand
Shake the pine torch

For now Junia marries Manlius—
Junia, such a one as Venus herself
Dwelling in Idalium,
She who came to the Phrygian judge,
A good maiden with a good omen

Part I: Ancient

Like the Asian myrtle
Shining forth on small flowering branches
Which the Hamadryad goddesses rear
With dewy moisture
As a toy for themselves.

Come now, Hymen, come,
Make your appearance,
Leave the Aonian grottoes of the Thespian rock
Which the nymph Aganippe makes cool
With showers from above.

Call to her home the mistress of the house,
Eager for her new husband.
Entwine her thoughts with love
As the clinging ivy, winding here and there,
Enmeshes the tree.

And you too, unwedded virgins,
For whom a like day will arrive,
Come at once and sing out,
Keeping the beat, "Oh Hymenaeus Hymen
Oh Hymen Hymenaeus"

So, hearing himself summoned
To his proper duty,
Hymen may more willingly come this way,
Guide to good Venus,
Coupler of good love.

What god is there
More to be sought by eager lovers?
Which of the heavenly ones shall men cherish
More greatly? Oh Hymenaeus Hymen
Oh Hymen Hymenaeus.

CATULLUS

To you, Hymen, the aging father prays
On behalf of his children;
For you, virgins unbind their garments;
For you the anxious new husband listens
With longing ear.

You yourself bring into the hands
Of the untamed youth
The blooming maiden from the bosom
Of her mother. Oh Hymenaeus Hymen
Oh Hymen Hymenaeus.

Without you, Venus cannot take the pleasure
Good tradition approves,
But she can if you are willing.
Who dares compare himself
To this god?

Without you, no house is able to produce children
Nor parent find support in offspring,
But they can if you are willing.
Who dares compare himself
To this god?

If a land lack your sacred rite,
It cannot produce soldiers to guard its borders,
But it can if you are willing.
Who dares compare himself
To this god?

Throw open the bolts of the door,
The bride is coming.
See how the torches shake their gleaming hair . . .

(21)

Part I: Ancient

Inborn modesty delays her . . .
Listening, she weeps
That she must go forth.

Cry no more, Aurunculeia,
There is no danger
That any woman more beautiful
Has ever witnessed bright day
Coming from the ocean.

Of such beauty is the hyacinth flower
Which stands high in the many-hued garden
Of the wealthy master.
But you delay. The day is passing.
Come forth, new bride.

Come forth, new bride,
If it pleases you now,
And listen to our words.
See how the torches shake their golden hair.
Come forth, new bride.

Your husband does not wish to trifle,
Committing unseemly acts
With some evil adultress,
Or to lie alone
Away from your soft breasts

But rather, as the pliant vine
Entwines the trees planted nearby,
So will he be entwined in your embrace.
But the day is passing.
Come forth, new bride.

Oh, bridal bed . . .
White-footed bed . . .

CATULLUS

How great are the joys to come for your lord,
Joys to be his in the wandering night
And at mid-day.
But the day is passing.
Come forth, new bride.

Boys, lift up the torches, for I see
The flame-hued wedding veil is coming.
Together, sing in measure
Io Hymen Hymenaeus Io
Io Hymen Hymenaeus.

Let the wanton fescennine jests
No longer be silent.
Let the *concubinus* not refuse nuts to the slaves
On hearing that his master
Has abandoned him.

Scatter the nuts to the slaves,
Lazy favorite,
You have played long enough.
It must please you now to serve Talassius.
Scatter the nuts.

A while ago the country wives
Did not interest you;
Now the barber shaves your cheeks,
Miserable, miserable one.
Scatter the nuts.

You, perfumed bridegroom,
People may say you are reluctant
To abstain from your former favorites,
But do abstain. Io Hymen Hymenaeus Io
Io Hymen Hymenaeus.

Part I: Ancient

We know you are acquainted with those things
Allowed to one alone,
But those same things are not allowed
To a husband. Io Hymen Hymenaeus Io
Io Hymen Hymenaeus.

You also, new bride, take care
Not to deny those favors
Which your husband seeks, lest he go elsewhere
To find them. Io Hymen Hymenaeus Io
Io Hymen Hymenaeus.

See how powerful and prosperous
The house of your husband is;
Let it serve you well.
Io Hymen Hymenaeus Io
Io Hymen Hymenaeus.

Even till that time when
White-haired old age with trembling head
Nods assent to everything for everybody.
Io Hymen Hymenaeus Io
Io Hymen Hymenaeus.

With good omen, lift your golden slippers
Across the threshhold
And enter within the polished door.
Io Hymen Hymenaeus Io
Io Hymen Hymenaeus.

Within, see how your husband reclines alone
On Tyrian couch,
Entirely intent on you.
Io Hymen Hymenaeus Io
Io Hymen Hymenaeus.

CATULLUS

In his inmost heart
The flame burns,
Not less than in yours
But more deeply. Io Hymen Hymenaeus Io
Io Hymen Hymenaeus.

Young attendant,
Let go the smooth arm of the girl,
Let her now enter her husband's room.
Io Hymen Hymenaeus Io
Io Hymen Hymenaeus.

You, good women,
Happily mated with old husbands,
Place the young girl on nuptial couch.
Io Hymen Hymenaeus Io
Io Hymen Hymenaeus.

Bridegroom, you may come to your wife
In bridal chamber,
Her face a bright flower,
White daisy—
Or flaming poppy.

But, young husband—so help me gods—
You are no less fair,
Nor does Venus neglect you.
But the day is passing.
Go then, do not linger.

You have not delayed long,
Already you are here.
May good Venus guide you,
Since openly you take your desires
And do not hide your good love.

Part I: Ancient

If anyone wishes to count
The many thousands of your pleasures,
Let him first add up the grains of sand
Of Africa, and the number of
The twinkling stars.

Enjoy your playing
And soon bring forth children.
So old a name
Should not be without children
But should always perpetuate its kind.

I pray that a little Torquatus,
Stretching forth his tender hand
From the bosom of his mother,
May smile sweetly at his father,
Tiny lips half-open.

Let him be like Manlius, his father,
Easily recognized by even those
Who don't know the relationship,
And may his resemblance to his father
Attest his mother's purity.

May the goodness of his mother
Shine in him and his descendants—
The best kind of inheritance,
Enduring like that of Telemachus
From his mother, Penelope.

Virgins, close the doors;
We have sung enough.
But you, good married couple,
Live happily, and in your marital duty
Employ your vigorous youth.

CATULLUS

A Debate on Marriage versus Virginity
Carmen 62

[SCENE: *A wedding feast, with a singing contest between a chorus of young men and a chorus of girls*]

Evening is coming, young men,
Stand up together,
Vesper at last barely shows
His long-awaited light in the sky.
Now it is time to stand up,
Now time to leave the fat tables,
Now the bride will come,
Now the nuptial song will be sung.
Hymen oh Hymenaeus, come, Hymen oh Hymenaeus.

Unmarried girls, do you see the young men?
Do stand up opposite them,
For certainly the Night Star now shows his fires
Over Mount Oeta.
Indeed, he does.
See how briskly the girls have risen.
It is not mere chance that they rise so readily:
They have something to sing worth our answering.
Hymen oh Hymenaeus, come, Hymen oh Hymenaeus.

MEN

No easy palm of victory is ours, fellows,
Look how the girls are mulling over
What they have composed.
They are not pondering for nothing,
For they have in their minds
Something worth remembering,

Part I: Ancient

And no wonder, for they work at it
And give their full minds to it,
Whereas we have let our minds wander one way,
And our ears another,
So, fairly enough, we may be defeated,
For victory loves diligence.
Anyway, now at least, turn your minds to the contest.
Soon the girls will begin to sing;
Soon it will be up to us to respond.
Hymen oh Hymenaeus, come, Hymen oh Hymenaeus.

The Contest Begins

GIRLS

Hesperus, what fire more cruel than yours
Moves across the sky?
For you are able to tear away the daughter
From the embrace of her mother,
To tear away the clinging daughter
From mother's embrace,
And give the chaste girl to ardent young man.
What more cruel thing than this do enemies commit
When a city is seized?
Hymen oh Hymenaeus, come, Hymen oh Hymenaeus.

MEN

Hesperus, what fire more delightful than yours
Shines in the sky?
For you with your flame make firm the marriages
Which have been pledged,
Which men and parents have plighted beforehand
But not joined
Until your flame has risen.
What gift of the gods is more longed-for

CATULLUS

Than this happy hour?
Hymen oh Hymenaeus, come, Hymen oh Hymenaeus.

GIRLS

Friends, Hesperus has stolen away one of our number . . .

MEN

At night thieves lie hidden
And many a time, Hesperus,
You apprehend in crime those same thieves
When you return in the morning,
The same star, with a changed name.
But unmarried girls like to carp at you
With feigned accusation:
But what if they carp at him they truly desire
In their secret thoughts?
Hymen oh Hymenaeus, come, Hymen oh Hymenaeus.

GIRLS

As a flower grows protected in a fenced garden
Unknown to cattle, torn by no plow,
Which the gentle breezes caress, the sun strengthens,
The rain brings to maturity,
Many boys, many girls desire it.
When the same flower wilts, plucked by sharp nail,
No boys, no girls desire it.
So it is with a virgin:
As long as she remains untouched,
So long is she cherished by her own.
When she has lost her chaste flower,
Her body defiled,
She remains neither pleasing to boys
Nor dear to girls.
Hymen oh Hymenaeus, come, Hymen oh Hymenaeus.

Part I: Ancient

MEN

As a mateless vine grows in vacant field,
Never lifting itself up, never producing mature grape,
Its tender body drooping with its own weight,
Topmost shoot almost touching root,
No farmers, no oxen tend it.
When by chance this same vine is joined to husband-elm,
Many farmers, many oxen tend it.
So it is with a virgin:
As long as she remains untouched,
So long does she grow old untended.
When at the ripe and proper time
She is matched in equal marriage,
She is more dear to her husband
And less distasteful to her father.
Hymen oh Hymenaeus, come, Hymen oh Hymenaeus.

And you, maiden,
Do not fight with such a husband.
It is not right to fight
With him to whom your father himself
Gave you in marriage—
Your father himself along with your mother
You must obey.
Hymen oh Hymenaeus, come, Hymen oh Hymenaeus.

Your virginity is not all your own—
In part it belongs to your parents:
A third part is your father's,
A third part is given to your mother,
Only a third part is yours.
Do not fight with two
Who have given their rights to son-in-law,
Together with the dowry.
Hymen oh Hymenaeus, come, Hymen oh Hymenaeus.

(30)

SENECA, 4 B.C.-A.D. 65
Translated by Ella Isabel Harris

Epithalamium for Murder
From *Medea*

IN THIS PLAY the nuptial song for Jason and his new wife, Creusa, is paralleled by the "dark" or "anti-"epithalamium of Medea, Jason's former wife, as she carries out her plan for murder and revenge.

As the play opens, Medea addresses the marriage gods but says she will pray instead to the powers of darkness and evil. Invoking Hell's king and queen and the Furies, she asks them to bring death to Jason's new bride, to their children, and to the bride's father, Creon. For Jason, Medea asks the gods of darkness to grant, not death, but what is worse, life—that he may suffer as an exile, hated, poor, and homeless. Her revengeful wish that Jason might beget sons like their father and daughters like herself is particularly ironic in that it echoes the conventional epithalamic wish made for the offspring of a happy bridal couple.

As evening comes, the chorus notes the arrival of Hesperus, the evening star, who traditionally heralds the approach of nuptial consummation. Near the end of the play, when Medea has slain one of her children and is about to kill the other, she crowns the horror with the triumphant announcement that through murder and revenge she has regained her "lost virginity" on this "glad nuptial day."

> Chaos of night eternal; realm opposed
> To the celestial powers; abandoned souls;
> King of the dusky realm; Persephone,
> By better faith betrayed; you I invoke,
> But with no happy voice. Approach, approach,
> Avenging goddesses with snaky hair,
> Holding in blood-stained hands your sulphurous torch!
> Come now as horrible as when of yore

Part I: Ancient

Ye stood beside my marriage bed; bring death
To the new bride, and to the royal seed,
And Creon. . . .

This still remains—for me to carry up
The marriage torches to the bridal room,
And, after sacrificial prayers, to slay
The victims on their altars. Seek, my soul—
If thou still livest, or if aught endures
Of ancient vigor—seek to find revenge
Through thine own bowels; throw off woman's fears. . . .

                        Evils unknown and wild
Hideous, frightful both to earth and heaven,
Disturb my soul—wounds, and the scattered corpse,
And murder. . . .

Gird thee with wrath, prepare thine utmost rage,
That fame of thy divorce may spread as far
As of thy marriage!

*   *   *

STATIUS, c. a.d. 45-96

Adapted from the prose translation of D. A. Slater

From *Epithalamium for Stella and Violentilla*
Why Do You Dally So?

VENUS COUNSELS THE MAIDEN:

Why do you dally so?
Would you stay shamefaced and unmated?
Do you not wish to bow to husband's yoke

STATIUS

Before your beauty dims?
Charms such as yours should not be idle,
These fleeting gifts are meant to be enjoyed.
I did not give you that proud brow
And spirit like my own
That you should pass the years unwed.

Here indeed is one whose heart is yours,
He is comely and renowned
And above all he worships you.
What man is there in Rome, what maid,
That has not heard this scholar-poet's songs?

Come then, become his bride.
Youth should not be wasted.
All nations and all hearts
I link with nuptial torch.
Birds and flocks and tribes of savage beasts
Do not disdain me.
The sky itself melts at my will
And weds with earth
As clouds break into showers.
So it is that in this world
All things beget their kind,
And thus is life renewed.

With these words Venus beguiled the maiden,
As into her secret heart the goddess breathed a
    thought
Of wedlock's glory.

Ah, Now I Know What Day This Is

The hills of Rome resound with solemn hymn
And torches wave with ritual flame

Part I: Ancient

As from far Helicon the Muses come
For the joining of the bridal.

Venus, mother of Aeneas,
Adorns the bride,
Whose eyes are downcast,
And leads her by the hand.
Venus directs the rites and decks the bridal bed
And chastens her own hair and gown
For the goddess must not outshine the girl.

The chorus sings for you, bridegroom,
Fling wide the doors,
The winged gods bring garlands.
With countless flowers
The Loves and Graces pelt you
And sprinkle subtle perfumes.
Roses, lilies, violets rain
And you become her shelter.

Truce, sweet bridegroom, to your sighing,
Kind Heaven grants your bliss.
Care and Fear, be gone,
Unbridled Love now yields to Law,
And Rumour is at peace.

No more will Juno ask Herculean chores
Or Fates assign you war with Hellish fiends;
The quest is ended now, the prize is yours
And loveless nights of old remain but dreams.

So comes the day for which the Fates
Had set up a snow-white skein—
The day on which the nuptials
Of Stella and Violentilla
Are to the world proclaimed.

STATIUS

Of the Night, Let the Bridegroom Sing

As day dawns bright by Heaven's grace,
The bridegroom walks the clouds
And roams the shining sky,
But it seems to him the stars stand still
And slow Aurora tarries.

Witnesses of the wooing,
The hills and shores and woods
Echo the bridal songs
While poet-friends bear gifts
To their loved fellow-bard.
One brings a lyre, one his wands,
And one the tawny skin of spotted deer.
One brings a quill to strike the lyre,
One rings the poet's brow with bays,
And one with Ariadne's crown.

The day has scarce begun
Amid auguries of bliss
When both homes are astir with festal company.
The gates are green with leaves,
The crossways bright with fire
And gay robes hedged about
With folk in plain attire.
The company envies man and maid,
But the bridegroom more.

In the gateway Hymen stands
Composing a new bridal song
To bewitch the poet-bridegroom.
Juno blesses the nuptial knot
And Concord unites the throng.

      Such is the wedding day.
      Of the night, let the bridegroom sing.

Part I: Ancient

Wishes for a Bridal Couple and Their Unborn Child

Soon may a noble offspring
Be born of you to Latium
To govern camp and courts
And create merry songs.

Cynthia, be thou kind,
Bless the tenth month with early fruit.
But, birth-goddess, be thou merciful,
Let the pledge not wound the parent.

Unborn child, spare your mother's tender frame,
And when Nature has in secret carved your brow,
May you be born with features like your father's
But like your mother more.

And you, dear bride, the fairest of the realm,
Cherish the bond your worthy lord
Has sought so long to knit.
May your beauty never lessen,
May your youthful ardor linger,
And your loveliness be slow to fade.

*   *   *

MARTIAL, c. a.d. 40-104
Translated by Garrett Stewart

For a Son's Marriage

Claudia Peregrina is marrying Pudens my son:
So bless them with your wedding torches, Hymen.

(36)

Rarest cinnamon with fragrant nard combines
    And Thesean honeycomb with Massic wines:
Vines do not more tightly clasp the elm, nor
    Lotus seek the water more, nor myrtle love the shore.
Let Concord rest perpetual in their bed, where
    Venus may forever guide so fairly yoked a pair:
May she love her husband even when the years have told,
    And may it never seem to him that she is also old.

* * *

AUSONIUS, c. 310-395
Translated by Garrett Stewart

To My Wife

Let us live, my wife, as we have lived, and keep
    The names we gave each other on the marriage bed:
Let time not change us in our coming age
    But let me stay your lover and you remain my bride
Even if I rival or exceed in years old Nestor
    And you surpass Deiphobe, Sibyl of Cumae,
Let us not remind each other we are growing old
    Nor enumerate our years more than their merits.

* * *

CLAUDIAN, c. 375-408
Adapted by Virginia Tufte from the prose translation of
Maurice Platnauer

CLAUDIAN, panegyrist of the Roman Emperor Honorius, in 398 wrote a 341-line epic for the marriage of Honorius and Maria, daughter of

(37)

Part I: Ancient

the general Stilicho, and accompanied the epic by four *fescennine* verses, a form of nuptial verse often bawdy or erotic, designed to frighten away the "evil eye" on man's most fortunate day. The epic opens with a description of the Emperor, wounded by Love and no longer interested in hunting, riding, or javelin-throwing. A long soliloquy by the tormented lover is followed by the laughter of Cupid, who hurries proudly to break the news to his mother, the goddess Venus. There follows a detailed description of Venus's Paradise, an enclosure rich in untended flowers, shady groves with birds chosen for the beauty of their songs, and trees that unite in love. Here are two fountains, one of honey and one of poison, in which Cupid dips his arrows. A thousand of his brother Loves frolic on the banks.

We are told that Cupid subdues the stars, the gods, and heaven, and that his brothers prey upon the common people. Also inhabiting the grove are other deities, among them License, Anger, Tears, Pallor, Boldness, Happy Fears, Pleasure, and Lovers' Oaths. Wanton Youth bars Age from the grove.

Cupid flies into the Paradise, to find Venus seated on her throne, with the three Graces occupied in dressing her hair. The poem ends with the wish that Maria's womb may grow big and a little Honorius may soon rest in his grandfather's lap.

The excerpts that follow have been titled by the editor. In the first, in Venus's Paradise, the union of trees is dramatized. In the second, the Graces attend Venus. In the third, Venus enjoins everyone to make love not war, and then—like an efficient mother-of-the-bride—takes charge of wedding preparations. Adornments of the nuptial chamber include spoils of war, some won in battles led by the bride's father.

From *Epithalamium for Honorius and Maria*

Palm Tree Mates with Palm

In this green countryside, the flowers bloom
Perpetually, untouched by laboring hand,
Content with Zephyr's care. No bird may come

Into its shady groves till Venus first
Has given her approval to its song.
The birds who please her flit among the trees—
The ones who fail the singing test must leave.
The very branches live for love, each tree
In its own time experiencing love's power.
The palm tree mates with palm, the poplar sighs
Its passion for its kind, the alder calls
To alder, and the plane to whispering plane.

The Hairdresser's Art

The Graces help the goddess dress her hair—
One pours a stream of nectar on her head,
One parts her locks with finest ivory comb,
The third with subtle art makes softest braid
And ringlets, taking care to leave untouched
A straying tress—such seeming disarray
The more becomes the fairest face.

Preparing for the Wedding

Away, my friends, with god of war and strife,
Give your devotion to my reign of love.
Drive out the horrid flash of sword and shield,
Silence the savage shouts, the battle cries,
Furl the banners—eagles, dragon's fire.
Today my standards wave upon the field.
Let flute instead of bugle sound. And festive lyre
Crowd from our halls war trumpet's blare.
Let kings now lay aside their power and pride
And mingle equally in happy throng.
May Joy be freed and grave Law unashamed
To join in this day's revelry.

Part I: Ancient

You, Hymen, prepare the wedding torches.
You, Graces, gather flowers for the feast.
You, Concord, weave twin garlands for the pair,
And you, my band of winged ones, be off
Wherever you can be of use. Not even the least
Should loaf. Go, some of you, and find the lamps
And make the brackets ready for the night.
Entwine door-posts with sacred myrtle boughs
And sprinkle nectar, some of you, about
The house, and kindle Sabacan incense.
The rest of you, arrange these China silks
And Sidon tapestries upon the ground.

With all your skill adorn the marriage bed,
Weave with gems its rich and ornate canopy.
Heap the gathered family wealth, the spoil
Honorius' grandsire won from Moor and Saxon,
All the emperor's father won in numerous wars,
With brave Stilicho general at his side.
On lofty couch display our triumphs' ware,
Barbaric splendor of kings' treasuries.
Let all our conquered wealth be gathered there.

Sing, Woods and Rivers All
From *Fescennine Verses in Honor of the Marriage of the Emperor Honorius*

Come, earth, wreathed now with nuptial spring,
   do honor to your master's marriage feast.

Sing, woods and rivers all,
   Sing, deep of ocean.

Give your blessing, too, Ligurian plains
   and yours Venetian hills.

Let Alpine heights now clothe themselves with roses
> and the fields of ice grow red.

Let the river Adige echo choric lays
> and meandering Mincius whisper gently through his reeds
> and Padus answer with his alders dripping amber.

Let Tiber's banks now ring with Roman voices
> and the golden city, rejoicing in the marriage of her lord,
> crown her seven hills with flowers.

Thorns Arm the Rose

The Evening Star appears above Idalium
And brings Love's blessing to the nuptial bed.
New bride is overcome by modesty
And girlish teardrops mark the crimson veil.
But do not cease, young man, your close attack,
With love, subdue opposing fingernail:
None can enjoy spring's perfumes or the honey
Of Hybla if he fears the scratch of thorn.
Thorns arm the rose and bees defend their sweets,
And difficulties but increase the joy . . .
The kiss is sweeter stolen through her tears.

May hands enlaced form tighter band than that
Between the ivy and the flowering tree
Or pliant vine and poplar. May kisses fall
In give and take of love to match the play
Of turtledoves. When lips have mingled souls
May you find calm in soft refreshing sleep.
May purple couch be warm with princely love,
And coverlets now bright with Tyrian dye

Part I: Ancient

Receive new emblem of victorious fight.
Let music of the flute ring out all night
And free the crowd from Law's severe restraints,
With license to indulge permitted jests.

* * *

ANONYMOUS, *7th or 8th century*

Hymn translated by Garrett Stewart

Epithalamium for the Dedication of a Church

Vision of peace, the blessed place Jerusalem,
Is raised in heaven out of living stones
And praised by angels as by attendants on a bride,
Newly arrived from heaven and ready
For the bed of wedlock with the Lord:
Her streets and walls are all of purest gold,
Her portals bright with pearl, and inner shrines lie open
To all who come by virtue of their worth
From sacrifice in Christ's name on this earth.

Her stones are hammered by enormous blows
And by the artificer's hand are fitted into place
To stay forever in the sacred edifice
Where Christ becomes the corner stone,
Contrived to fasten and unite the walls
And fix the city Sion by her faith in him,
The sacred city cherished of the Lord,
One plenitude of measured melodies and praise,
One tribute to the unity and trinity of God.

ANONYMOUS

At our entreaty enter here the temple, Lord,
Receive our voiceless pleas in your sweet mercy,
And pour abundant blessing over them;
May all deserve an answer to their prayers,
To share the great attainment of the saints,
To enter into Paradise and be carried to their rest.
Glory and immortal honor to the Lord all high;
To God the Father, God the Son, and to the Holy
    Ghost
Be there praise and dominion in this and every age.

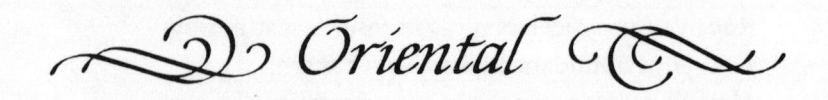

Oriental

From the NIHON SHOKI
Translated from the Japanese by Donald L. Philippi

Dawn Song (A.D. 513)

THIS SONG celebrates the marriage in A.D. 513 of the Imperial Prince Magari no Ohine (later Emperor Ankan) and Princess Kasuga, but it is a variant of a type that was apparently widely distributed. This version comes from the *Nihon shoki*, a collection which includes many popular songs, but a similar song is found in the *Manyōshū*, the first great anthology of Japanese literary poetry.

In many European nuptial poems, the embracing lovers are compared to trees with interwoven branches or to a vine clinging to an elm. In this Japanese song, the bridegroom compares the embrace to the mingling and entwining of vines. In European poems, choruses of birds or human singers often exchange songs to celebrate the wedding day, and sometimes the chorus returns the following morning at dawn to awaken the couple. In this Japanese song, an exchange between "the bird of the yard" and "the bird of the field" awakens the couple at dawn, and the bridegroom himself bursts into song.

> Unable to find a wife
>   In the land of the eight islands,
> Hearing that
>   In the land of Kasuga
> Of the spring sunshine,
>   There was a fair maiden,
> Hearing that
>   There was a good maiden:

>   The doors of wood
>   Of flourishing *hi* trees—
>   Pushing them open,
>   I entered
>   And embraced her legs,
>   Taking her as wife,
>   And embraced her head,
>   Taking her as wife,
>   Letting my beloved's hands
>   Embrace me,
>   And embracing my beloved
>   With my hands,
>   Like clinging vines,
>   Mingling and entwining—
>
>   Just then,
>   When I was sleeping well,
>   The bird of the yard,
>   The cock crowed,
>   The bird of the field,
>   The pheasant resounded.
>
>   Already, before even telling
>   Of my love,
>   The day has dawned, my beloved.

* * *

From the KOJIKI

Translated from the Japanese by Donald L. Philippi

Metal Hoe Hill (c. A.D. 450)

IT MAY HAVE BEEN an old custom for the bride to run and hide; such a marriage custom is recorded in parts of Okinawa. When Emperor

Part I: Ancient

Yūryaku went to Kasuga to marry Odo-hime, daughter of the ruler of the Wani clan, the girl ran away and hid on a hill, and the Emperor composed this song. After that time, the hill was called "Metal Plough Hill." This song is taken from the *Kojiki*, the great chronicle of Japanese myth, legend, songs, and historical data completed in A.D. 712.

> The hill
> Where the maiden is hiding—
> Oh for five hundred
> Metal hoes:
> How I would dig it up!

* * *

From THE BOOK OF SONGS, c. 800-600 B.C.

Translated from the Chinese by Arthur Waley [1]

To the Lady of Ch'i

> Here they gallop pak, pak,
> Bamboo awning, red leatherwork.
> The Lu road is easy and wide;
> A lady of Ch'i sets out at dusk.
>
> Four black horses well-groomed,
> Dangling reins all glossy.
> The Lu road is easy and wide;
> All happiness to this lady of Ch'i!

[1] All titles in this group have been supplied by the editor.

The waters of the Wên stretch broad;
The escort has splendid steeds.
The Lu road is easy and wide;
A pleasant journey to the lady of Ch'i!

The waters of the Wên rush headlong;
The escort has swift steeds.
The Lu road is easy and wide;
Good love-sport to the lady of Ch'i!

Companion of Her Lord till Death

Companion of her lord till death,
The pins of her wig with their six gems,
Easy and stately,
Like a mountain, a river
Worthy of her blazoned gown.
That our lady is not a fine lady
How can any man say?

Gorgeous in its beauty
Is her pheasant-wing robe,
Her thick hair billows like clouds,
No false side-lock does she need.
Ear-plugs of jade,
Girdle pendants of ivory,
Brow so white.
How comes it that she is like a heavenly one,
How comes it that she is like a god?

Oh, splendid
In her ritual gown!
Rich the crapes and embroideries
That she trails and sweeps.

Part I: Ancient

Clear is our lady's brow,
That brow well-rounded.
Truly such a lady
Is a beauty matchless in the land.

Of Silk Is Her Fishing-Line

IN THE CHINESE SONGS, as in European nuptial poems, fish are symbols of fertility and blessings. In several parts of the world, fish are included in various ways in the marriage ritual. Bride and bridegroom in some parts of India go into the water up to their knees and catch fish in a new garment; a rite of this kind may have existed in ancient China. The fish which are caught indicate that Heaven will bless the couple with children and prosperity.

Gorgeous in their beauty
Are the flowers of the cherry,
Are they not magnificent in their dignity,
The carriages of the royal bride?

Gorgeous in her beauty
As flower of peach or plum,
Granddaughter of King P'ing,
Child of the Lord of Ch'i.

Wherewith does she angle?
Of silk is her fishing-line,
This child of the Lord of Ch'i,
Granddaughter of King P'ing.

In the Wicker Fish-Trap

AN ASSORTMENT of omens and portents appears in both European and Oriental nuptial poetry. The crowing of the cock and the sounds made by other birds assume special significance.

In the wicker fish-trap by the bridge
Are fish, both bream and roach.
A lady of Ch'i goes to be married;
Her escort is like a trail of clouds.

In the wicker fish-trap by the bridge
Are fish, both bream and tench.
A lady of Ch'i goes to be married;
Her escort is thick as rain.

In the wicker fish-trap by the bridge
The fish glide free.
A lady of Ch'i goes to be married;
Her escort is like a river.

Wind and Rain

Wind and rain, chill, chill!
But the cock crowed kikeriki.
Now that I have seen my lord,
How can I fail to be at peace?

Wind and rain, oh, the storm!
But the cock crowed kukeriku.
Now that I have seen my lord,
How can I fail to rejoice?

Wind and rain, dark as night,
The cock crowed and would not stop.
Now that I have seen my lord,
How can I any more be sad?

Fast Bundled Is the Firewood

Fast bundled is the firewood;
The Three Stars [1] have risen.

[1] The Belt of Orion.

Part 1: Ancient

Is it to-night or which night
That I see my Good Man?
Oh, masters, my masters,[1]
What will this Good Man be like?

Fast bundled is the hay;
The Three Stars are at the corner.[2]
Is it to-night or which night
That shall see this meeting?
Oh, masters, my masters,
What will that meeting be like?

Fast bundled is the wild-thorn;
The Three Stars are at the door.
Is it to-night or which night
That I see that lovely one?
Oh, masters, my masters,
What will that lovely one be like?

Thick Grows the Tarragon

Thick grows the tarragon
In the centre of that slope.
I have seen my lord;
He was pleased and courteous to boot.

Thick grows the tarragon
In the middle of that island.
I have seen my lord,
And my heart is glad.

Thick grows the tarragon
In the centre of that mound.

---

[1] May merely be a meaningless exclamation.
[2] Of the house, as seen from inside.

HAN DYNASTY

> I have seen my lord;
> He gave me a hundred strings of cowries.
>
> Unsteady is that osier boat;
> It plunges, it bobs.
> But now that I have seen my lord
> My heart is at rest.

*   *   *

Selections from the
HAN DYNASTY, 206 B.C.-A.D. 221
English versions by David Rafael Wang

Ancient Quatrain

IN CHINESE and Japanese poetry mandarin ducks are symbols of conjugal felicity.

> On the southern mountain: a cassia tree
> And on its branch: a pair of mandarin ducks
> Necking with each other all year round
> Their love makes them forget all time.

Marriage Vow

> O, celestial beings
> Let our feelings for each other
> continue without diminishing
> Only when mountains are leveled
> to basins, when ocean waters run
> dry, when winter is ripped
> with thunders, when the summer sky
> rains snow, and heaven and earth

Part I: Ancient

are smashed together, shall we
ever dare to be parted!

Up the Mountain to Pick Mawu

IN ANCIENT CHINA *mawu* was considered a spice as well as an herb to induce fertility. In this folk song, the old wife is bringing the herb for the husband's bride.

I climbed the mountain to pick *mawu*
I climbed down to visit my spouse
Kneeling long, I asked my former husband:
"How is your second wife?"

"My new wife is pretty good
But she can't compare with the old.
I'm not complaining about her features
But she's less handy at work."

"When your new wife came thru the main gate,
Your old woman left thru the back door."

"The new wife weaves yellow silk,
The old wove white gauze.
She puts out forty feet per day
You put out fifty feet and more.
Compare the yellow with the white silk,
The new—not quite as good as the old."

ANCIENT CHINESE

LIU HSI-CHUN, c. 110 B.C.
English version by David Rafael Wang

Song of Grief

To APPEASE HUNS, Tartars, and other northern "barbarians," it was customary for the emperors of the Han Dynasty (206 B.C.-A.D. 221) to send Chinese princesses in marriage to the khans or chieftains. However, the so-called princesses were usually beauties selected by the imperial court from villages all over China. Liu Hsi-chun, the poetess, was sent between 110-105 B.C. as a Chinese princess to wed the Khan of Wu Sun in present-day Sinkiang.

> My family married me to the other end of the world
> Far far away in the alien land to the Prince of Sinkiang
> With a Mongol hut as my house and felt as my walls
> With meat as constant diet and koumiss as my drink
> Thinking of my homeland often my heart is torn
> May I fly back as a yellow crane to visit my home!

* * *

From ANCIENT CHINESE Writing
English versions by David Rafael Wang

Blues #8

> Frailly, frailly stands the lone bamboo
> With its root deep in the cove of the mountain

(53)

Part I: Ancient

Once wedded to you, my husband,
I shall be constant as the *t'u szu*
The *t'u szu* has its time of growing,
A couple, their time of meeting.
Thousand miles overcome, we had our wedding,
But sadly are we separated by mountains.
Thinking of you makes me feel old
When will your coach ever return?
I feel lost as the marsh orchid
Who enjoys a brief season of full splendor
But withers with the autumn grass
When left, for a long time, unplucked.
As long as you are lofty and untainted,
What complaints have I to register?

Poem #18

A guest came from faraway
Left me a yard of embroidered silk
Ten thousand miles apart,
My husband's heart is unchanged.
On the silk: a pair of mandarin ducks
What a coverlet it would make!
To use it for remembrance
I shall tighten the stitches again
Once our love is cemented
Let no parting break!

* * *

TU FU, 712-770

English version by David Rafael Wang

The Newlyweds' Separation

The dodder leans   against the rubus
Parasitic   cannot grow long
A girl married to   a soldier-husband
Just a weed   discarded on the road.
Hair barely bound   as your wife
The straw mat on your bed   not yet warm
Evening wedding and   dawn separation
Why—oh why—   such a rush to be off?
Not far away do you   have to travel
To the border   at River's South
Ritual not   fully consummated,
Should I go   before my in-laws?
When my parents   were bringing me up
They warned me   against a roving life
Every girl has   her day   of wedlock
Even dogs and chickens   know their roost.
You are going   to the fields strewn with corpses
How can I not feel   a pang inside?
Though I would   swear to follow you
I fear that   green will turn yellow.
Don't worry about   your nuptials
Keep your mind   on duties alone!
If a woman appears   among soldiers
The men lose   their fighting spirit.
Because I was   a poor girl
It took ages   to prepare my wardrobe
My wardrobe   cannot be repeated

Part I: Ancient

Facing you, I wash   my makeup off.
I lift my head and   watch the birds flying
Each with two wings   regardless of size
Human life has   endless complications—
Let thinking of you   be enough!

           *   *   *

WANG CHIEN, c. 775
English version by David Rafael Wang

The Newlyweds' Cuisine

The third night after wedding
    I get near the stove.

Rolling up my sleeves
    I make a fancy broth.

Not knowing the taste
    of my mother-in-law,

I try it first upon her
    youngest girl.

CHU CHING-YÜ, *born* 797
English version by David Rafael Wang

The Toilette

On my wedding night
> I arrange the red candlesticks

Waiting for the morning
> to wait on my in-laws.

After my toilette
> I whisper to my husband:

"Have I penciled my eyebrows
> sharply enough?"

PART II
Medieval to Early Renaissance

There is a sumptuous variety in Part Two. It includes three poems by the great medieval Hebrew poet, Judah Halevi, born in Toledo, Spain; two of the earliest nuptial poems in English, both by poet-priests, John Lydgate and William Dunbar; extracts from the Latin of the great Renaissance scholar Erasmus of Rotterdam; extracts from the Latin of the Italian epic poet Ariosto; and a translation of the sensuous Latin *Basia* (*Kisses*) of the Dutch poet Johannes Secundus. The section concludes with two short Chinese poems, one by Yu Ch'ien, and the other by T'ang Yin, nicknamed "Elder Tiger," renowned as both poet and painter.

One of the liveliest motifs in the period is the marriage versus virginity argument. Debates on this subject appear in classical times (as in Catullus's Carmen 62), in the Middle Ages, and in the early Renaissance as well. In the classical epithalamium, the argument is won by the defenders of marriage. In medieval ascetic epithalamia—poems that celebrate mystical unions—the argument is won by the champions of virginity. But even in the Middle Ages a few strong advocates of marriage are heard, one of the most memorable being Chaucer's Wife of Bath. Schooled by five husbands and looking for a sixth, the Wife insisted that God bade man "to wax and multiply" and argued that it was self-defeating for even the champions of virginity to oppose marriage:

> *And certes, if ther were no seed ysowe,*
> *Virginitee, thanne wherof sholde it growe?*

About a century after Chaucer, a similar argument was presented in a very different way when one of the most eloquent defenses of marriage in European literature was written by the gentle priest and humanist, Erasmus of Rotterdam, in the form of a 24-page Latin "Epistle to Persuade a Young Gentleman to Marriage." Shortly after Erasmus's death, the epistle was translated into English by Thomas Wilson and widely circulated in the many editions of his book, *The Art of Rhetoric*. Erasmus's arguments appear to have influenced many English poets, including Shakespeare.

Erasmus argues that marriage was instituted by God and renewed after the flood; he cites Biblical passages expressing approval of marriage, and also quotes Plutarch, Augustus Caesar, Juvenal, and other authorities. Matrimony is natural, he contends, and it would be a foul thing if beasts could observe the laws of nature and man could not. It is through physical intercourse that men make their kind immortal. He quotes Pliny on the subject of marriage among trees: the husband tree leans with his boughs, as if he would desire intercourse with the women trees growing round about him. And he quotes Pliny and other authors who think that male and female exist in all things that the earth yields, including precious stones. The sky or firmament, Erasmus says, "doth play the part of a husband, while it puffeth up the earth, the mother of all things, and maketh it fruitful with casting seed upon it."

The man who has no mind for marriage, Erasmus writes, is "no man but rather a stone, an enemy to nature, a rebel to God himself, seeking through his own folly, his . . . destruction." For the devout, virginity "is a heavenly thing," but "wedlock is a manly thing." And Erasmus asks, perhaps rather wistfully:

> *What can be more pleasant than to live with a wife,*
> *matched together both in heart and mind,*
> *in body and soul, sealed together*
> *with the bond and league of a holy sacrament,*
> *a sweet mate in your youth,*
> *a thankful comfort in your age.*

JUDAH HALEVI, 1085?-1140

Translated by Ephriam Sando and Rabbi William Cutter

JUDAH HALEVI, though he wrote in Hebrew, was influenced by the Spanish culture around him. He was the author of many wedding odes and songs of friendship, some of which echo the imagery of the *Song of Solomon*.

To the Choice Bridegroom

Hail the choice groom—
Hail to his friends and true companions.
The greeting of a friend traverses the distance with his
    eyes:
His heart looks across face to face.
When two children of good birth are joined—
Noble scions, sprigs of pleasantness—
Their faces gleam through the marriage canopy
Like stars through a braiding of clouds.

Amid the Myrtles

The bridal deer stand amid the myrtles,
Conferring clear myrrh beyond boundaries.
The myrtle throbs for the gladness of their fragrance
And folds his wings like a cherub over them.
The myrtle imagines of entering their fragrance,
But the spicery of their savor entrances his scent.

Part II: Medieval to Early Renaissance

To the Bridegroom

Be glad, O youth, in your young manhood
And reap the fruit of your gladness,
You and the bride of your youth
Who comes into your house.

Valued blessings of the One
Draw together upon your head,
Your house at peace from fear;
All who threaten you shall be lost.
When you lie down, you will not fear:
Sweet will be your sleep.

Flourish in your honor, bridegroom.
Offer up and send forth your glory
That God may pierce the heart of your enemies;
He will forgive the failings of your youth
And bless you in all that your hand
Sends forth and gathers in.

Remember your Rock and your Maker
Even when His goodness comes.
Mortality shall get you;
For as your days, so shall be your strength.
Be blessed in your coming in
And be blessed in your going out.

Let your word be with the chosen upright
That you catch wisdom wherever you turn,
That your house be sure;
When you call out "Peace," God shall reply.
Your dwelling shall be peace, and your covenant
With the stones of the field.

Your greatness shall rise, and not delay.
And He shall call you; you shall He choose.
Then your sun at the night and the dawn
Shall pierce through like the dawn
And to you from the womb of the dawn
Is the dew of your youth.

* * *

JOHN LYDGATE, c. 1370-1451

From *Epithalamium for Gloucester*

JOHN LYDGATE's "balade" of almost 200 lines written in 1422 for the marriage of Humphrey, Duke of Gloucester, and Jacqueline, Countess of Holland, Zealand, and Hainault, bears little resemblance to the Sappho-Catullan nuptial lyric but stands rather in the tradition of the Statius-Claudian rhetorical epithalamium. Its main theme is the wish that by means of the marriage, harmony and peace may be attained between Holland and England. The poet declares that wars and the fall of kings are predetermined by the stars, but God is able to go counter to the stars and to bring peace through the institution of marriage. It is not only the Christian God who sanctions such union, the poet-priest tells us, but Cupid, Venus, and Nature herself also regard marriage favorably. Books and ancient chronicles, he argues, give examples of the benefits of marriage, for they tell

> Howe maryages / have grounde and cause be
> Betwene landes / of pees and unytee.

The poet expresses the hope that this marriage will bring

> A nuwe sonne / to shynen of gladnesse
> In boothe londes / texcluden al derknesse

Part II: Medieval to Early Renaissance

>Of oolde hatred and of al rancour
>Brought in by meene / of oon that is the floure
>Thoroughe oute the world / called of wommanheed
>Truwe ensaumple and welle of al goodenesse
>Benyngne of poorte / roote of goodelyheed
>Soothefast myrrour of beaute and fayrnesse.

In his extravagant praise of the bridegroom, the poet compares him to assorted mythological, Biblical, and more recent historical figures:

>With Salamoun hathe he sapyence
>ffaame of knighthoode / with Cesar Julius
>Of rethoryk and / eeke of eloquence
>Equypollent with Marcus Tulius.

The poet concludes with a prayer to the Christian god that there may be peace, an appeal to Hymen and Juno for blessings, and an apology to the bride ("the goodely fresshe duchesse") for his inadequacy as a poet. The poem is too long and too dull to be reproduced in its entirety in this book, but the extracts give the reader some idea of the nature of this very early English wedding poem.

*   *   *

WILLIAM DUNBAR, c. 1460-1520

From *The Thrissil and the Rois*

ALTHOUGH the wedding of James IV and Princess Margaret Tudor took place in August 1503, the poem was written earlier and has a spring setting, sparkling with what C. S. Lewis has called the "May morning note" of some of the late Latin nuptial poems. It is a nature allegory, too long to be printed here, but the following extracts and summary will give some idea of what it is like.

> Quehn Merche wes with variand windis past,
> And Appryll had, with hir silver schouris,
> Tane leif at nature with ane orient blast;
> And lusty May, that muddir is of flouris,
> Had maid the birdis to begyn thair houris
> Among the tendir odouris reid and quhyt,
> Quhois armony to heir it wes delyt;
> In bed at morrow, sleiping as I lay,
> Me thocht Aurora, wih hir cristall ene,
> In at the window lukit by the day,
> And halsit me, with visage paill and grene;
> On quhois hand a lark sang fro the splene,
> Awalk, luvaris, out of your slomering,
> Se how the lusty morrow dois up spring.

The poet, after being awakened by Aurora, is ordered by the Month of May to write something in her honor and to describe the "Ros of most plesance." In the beautiful garden of the dream vision, Dame Nature summons the beasts, birds, and flowers to receive her commands. The poet takes his allegorical devices from heraldry, the bridegroom being represented by the Lion, whom Dame Nature crowns as king of beasts. On the Royal Arms of Scotland he is portrayed

> Rycht strong of corpis, of fassoun fair but feir,
> Lusty of schaip, lycht of deliverance,
> Reid of his cullour, as is the ruby glance;
> On feild of gold he stude full mychtely,
> With flour delycis sirculit lustely.

The main symbol for the bridegroom, however, is the thistle of Scotland, and for the bride the Tudor rose, which mingles the red rose of Lancaster and the white rose of York.

Dame Nature gives the "awfull Thrissill" a crown of rubies because he is an able warrior, and sends him forth as a champion, with the instructions:

> And, sen thow art a king, thow be discreit;
> Herb without vertew thow hald nocht of sic pryce
> As herb of vertew and of odor sueit;
> And lat no nettill vyle, and full of vyce
> Hir fallow to the gudly flour delyce;
> Nor latt no wyld weid, fullof churlichenes,
> Compair hir till the lilleis nobilnes.
>
> Not hald non udir flour in sic denty
> As the fresche Ros of cullour reid and quhyt;
> For gife thow dois, hurt is thyne honesty,
> Conciddering that no flour is so perfyt,
> So full of vertew, plesans, and delyt,
> So full of blisfull angeilik bewty,
> Imperiall birth, honour and dignite."

The Rose is crowned as queen of flowers, and the flowers and songbirds join in exuberant rejoicing and welcome to the princess, concluding with a prayer that Christ may protect her from all adversity. Awakened by the singing, the poet composes his song:

> And thus I wret, as ye haif hard to forrow,
> Off lusty May upone the nynt morrow.

* * *

ERASMUS, c. 1466-1536

Translated from the Latin by Nathaniel Bailey, 1733

Sweet Temper and Mutual Affection

IN ONE OF *The Familiar Colloquies*, Erasmus includes a nuptial song for Petrus Aegidius and his bride Cornelia, but the dialogue that precedes the song is of more interest than the song itself. Alipius, a discerning man, is talking with the Muses and Graces. The Muses praise bride and bridegroom and mention that they will sing and the Graces will dance. They give a prescription for happy marriage.

MUSES

They will not only dance, but they will also unite those two true Lovers, with the indissoluble Ties of mutual Affection, that no Difference or Jarring shall ever happen between 'em. She shall never hear anything from him, but my Life; nor he from her, but my Soul. . . .

ALIPIUS

But I have known a great many, to whom these kind Words have been chang'd into the quite contrary, in less than three Months Time; and instead of pleasant Jests at Table, Dishes and Trenchers have flown about. The Husband, instead of my dear Soul, has been called Blockhead, Toss-pot, Swill-tub; and the Wife, Sow, Fool, dirty Drab.

MUSES

You say very true; but these Marriages were made when the Graces were out of Humour: But in this Marriage, a Sweetness of Temper will always maintain a mutual Affection.

ALIPIUS

Indeed you speak of such a happy Marriage as is very seldom seen.

MUSES

An uncommon Felicity is due to such uncommon Virtues.

Part II: Medieval to Early Renaissance

ARIOSTO, 1474-1533

Translated from the Latin by Birgitta Wohl and Virginia Tufte

From "Song for the Third Marriage of Lucrezia Borgia"

FOR THE MARRIAGE in 1501 of Lucrezia Borgia and Alphonso d'Este, son of the Duke of Ferrara, elaborate celebrations were held in both Rome and Ferrara. Ariosto's poem, one of many written for the occasion, portrays the arrival of the bride and her train of Roman attendants in Ferrara, with a singing contest (in the manner of Catullus's Carmen 62) between the young men of Ferrara, welcoming her to the city, and the young men of Rome, who lament that Rome has again fallen into ruin at the loss of their "pulcherrima virgo."

>   Rise up! the flute sounds in the distance
>   To tell us the bride is coming.
>   See, she is coming,
>   As shapely as Venus,
>   Swan-drawn goddess, revisiting Memphis or high Cythera
>   Or the grove of Ida or the temples of Amathous.
>
>   Do you notice how Charis (tiniest of fairies)
>   Hovers about the virgin so praised?
>   Light wings breathe gently
>   On sweet lips and eyes, shoulder and cheek,
>   Beauty serene.
>
>   Do you notice how Cupids playfully clamour
>   And pour on her hair their baskets of flowers?
>   With lilies like snowflakes one touches her brow,
>   Another her cheek with radiant roses

ARIOSTO

And amaranths unfading.
The tender Loves flutter in wonder
At beauty outshining their colorful tokens.

Do you notice how the young men of Latium,
Who will soon return to their homes,
Follow the carriages, brows wrinkled in thought?
Why do we not listen to what they are pondering,
Their voices low,
And consider how we can return
Some witty and appropriate words
In the way of a wedding song.
>   Sweet Hymen, joyful Hymen,
>   Come, O Hymenaeus.

THE YOUNG MEN OF ROME

Look at the Herculean young men
Who advance against us.
Oh, friends, have they already prepared
For a singing match?
Certainly they do not approach in this fashion
Without purpose.
Victory will be very difficult for us
For bridal songs require happy hearts,
And we are sad.
What can we do but pronounce something sorrowful,
Thrust down from the height as we are,
Because foreign bridal beds are stealing you from us,
Most beautiful Lucretia.
>   Hard Hymen, Hymenaeus,
>   Hostile toward the pious Latins!

THE YOUNG MEN OF FERRARA

Look at the Roman poets;
Although now they are in want of a well-prepared song,

Part II: Medieval to Early Renaissance

They have often before adorned their heads
With the crown of victory.
Therefore, friends, we who must stand first
In this contest of songs
Shall not easily win.
But greater is the glory
Born from much toil.
Set your minds on this, friends,
Concentrate, so there will be no delay
When our time comes to sing
Our learned song.
> Sweet Hymen, Joyful Hymen,
> Come, O Hymenaeus.

THE YOUNG MEN OF ROME

Everything has been turned upside down.

Once most powerful Rome lifted its head
Among the Ausonian cities as high
As the aged silver-fir among the graceful broom-plants
Or as the old Tiber among tiny rivulets;
Then the achievements of men's minds were as brilliant
As ramparts were high.

Now Rome is empty and deserted,
Pressed down,
And where the lofty temples of the gods
And the Capitolium were,
And the Curia and the benches worn by the holy Senate,
There now with crooked foot the ivy grows,
And malicious bushes,
Shameful lurking-places for malevolent serpents.

But even this loss is slight:
Everything that is left might fall,

ARIOSTO

And life could be lived in bare caves
If only it remained possible to keep you with us,
Most beautiful virgin.
>Hard Hymen, Hymenaeus,
>Hostile toward the pious Latins!

THE YOUNG MEN OF FERRARA

Everything has been turned upside down.

Once Ferrara was poor, with modest ramparts,
Surrounded by the green bank on this side
And the muddy marsh on the other,
Possessing but scanty riches and tiny houses
And small temples of the gods,
Suitable then for an insignificant people
And a weak Senate.

Now Ferrara rises above neighboring cities
As the father Apennines among the hills of Bacchus,
Or the Po among the rivers which it receives.
The places where little boats fished,
Or nets dried in sunny field,
Now are embellished by regal temples,
Houses, forums, crossroads, courts, and towers,
And Herculean walls, gates, and roads.

Even all this is hardly great enough for its people,
Now through high disposition and devotion to learning
Able to challenge the offspring of Mars.
And Ferrara can boast of no greater glory
Than to receive you as its mistress,
Most beautiful virgin.
>Sweet Hymen, joyful Hymen,
>Come, O Hymenaeus.

Part II: Medieval to Early Renaissance

THE YOUNG MEN OF ROME

Hard Hymen, Hymenaeus, hostile to the pious Latins,
You who have power to snatch away the trembling girl
From the tears of her poor parents
And give her to a husband burning with desire,
And lead her far from her native country
To distant coasts,
Hard Hymen, Hymenaeus, hostile to the pious Latins.

THE YOUNG MEN OF FERRARA

Sweet Hymen, joyful Hymen, come O Hymenaeus,
You who aim to join the longing girl
With the longing young man,
And feel compassion for the silent plaints of the lovers;
You who do not allow a girl to languish in empty bed
But join distant cities in nuptial compact,
Sweet Hymen, joyful Hymen, come O Hymenaeus.

. . . . . .

And now, Romulean poets, do not strive longer against
 us,
Our singing match has come to an end.
Let us enter the royal house
Let it be our pleasure
To join in a song of concord.
        Sweet Hymen, joyful Hymen,
        Come, O Hymenaeus.

JOHANNES SECUNDUS, 1511-1536
Translated from the Latin by George Ogle, 1731

Epithalamium

JOHANNES SECUNDUS is the Latin name of the Dutch poet Jan Everaerts, who died before he was twenty-five but whose Latin *Basia (Kisses)* has caused him to be remembered as one of the world's great writers of sensuous love lyrics. His epithalamium, a glowing and voluptuous description of the joys of conjugal love, is here presented in a popular eighteenth-century translation.

>The hour is come, with pleasure crowned,
>Borne in eternal order round!
>Hour, of endearing looks and smiles,
>Hour, of voluptuous sports and wiles,
>Hour, fraught with fondly-murmuring sighs,
>Hour, blest with softly dying eyes,
>Hour, with commingling kisses sweet,
>Hour, of transporting bliss replete,
>Hour, worthy ev'n of gods above,
>Hour, worthy all-commanding Jove!
>For not a fairer-omened hour
>Could promise the kind Cnidian power;
>Not tender Cupid could bestow,
>The boy with silver-splendid bow
>And golden wing, delicious boy,
>That sorrow still allays with joy;
>Nor, wont at nuptials to preside,
>She that of Jove is sister-bride;
>Nor he, on tuneful summit born,
>The God whom flowery wreaths adorn,

Who blooming beauty tears away,
Bears off by force the charming prey;
From the reluctant mother tears,
To the rapacious lover bears.
Hour long desired! hour long delayed!
Thrice happy youth! thrice happy maid!

Thrice happy youth, supremely blest,
Of every wish in one possest!
To thee, the maid of form divine
Comes seeming loth, but inly thine:
Such form as Juno's self might choose,
Nor yet the martial maid refuse;
Though that th' aetherial sceptre sways,
And this the shining shield displays:
Nor yet the Cyprian queen disdain,
But, to re-seek the Phrygian swain
And cause of beauty re-decide
In shady vale of flowering Ide,
How sure to gain the golden prize,—
Though judged by less discerning eyes,—
She, in that matchless form arrayed:
Thrice happy youth! thrice happy maid!

Thrice happy maid, supremely blest,
Of every wish in one possest!
To thee, on wings of love and truth,
Comes, all devote, the raptured youth,
Thy bending neck with eager hold,
Thy waist impatient to enfold;
While, for that hair of easy flow,
While, for that breast of virgin snow,
While, for that lip of rosy dye,
While, for that sweetly-speaking eye,

JOHANNES SECUNDUS

With silent passion he expires
And burns with still-consuming fires,
Now Phoebus, slow to quit the skies,
Now loitering Phoebus, slow to rise,
Persists alternate to upbraid!
Thrice happy youth! thrice happy maid!

Spare, youth, your vows, vain offerings spare:
Forbear your needless sighs, forbear:
Lo! Time, in ever-varying race,
Brings on at last the wished-for space.
Mild Venus, with propitious ears,
The sorrows of her votaries hears;
While Cynthius, down the western steeps,
Low plunges in Iberian deeps,
And quits the ample fields of air
To his night-wandering sister's care:
Than whom no light more grateful shines
To souls which mutual love conjoins;
Not he that leads the stars along,
Brightest of all the glittering throng,
Hesper, with golden torch displayed:
Thrice happy youth! thrice happy maid!

See where the maid all panting lies,
Ah! never more a maid to rise,
And longs, yet trembles at thy tread,
Her cheeks perfused with decent red,
Expressing-half her inward flame,
Half-springing from ingenuous shame:
Tears from her eyes perhaps may steal,
Her joys the better to conceal;
Then sighs, with grief unreal fraught,
Then follow plaints of wrongs un-thought.

But cease not thou, with idle fears,
For all her plaints, or sighs, or tears:
Kissed be the tears from off her eyes;
With tender murmurs stopped, her sighs;
With soothings soft her plaints allayed:
Thrice happy youth! thrice happy maid!

The maid, in decent order placed,
With every bridal honour graced,
Through all her limbs begin to spread
The glowings of the genial bed
And languid sleep dispose to take,
Did not the youth, more watchful, wake;
And the mild Queen of fierce desire
With warmth not disproportioned fire.
Taught hence, nor purpled kings to prize,
Nor sceptred Jove that rules the skies,
Soon for soft combats he prepares,
And gentle toils of amorous wars:
Declared, but with no loud alarms,
Begun, but with no dreaded arms:
Kisses, which, wanton as he strays,
He darts a thousand wanton ways
At mouth, or neck, at eyes, or cheeks;
Him humbly she full oft bespeaks,
Entreats, an helpless maid to spare,
And begs with trembling voice, "forbear";
Full oft his rudeness loudly blames;
His boundless insolence proclaims;
His lips with lips averse withstands;
With hands restrains his roving hands:
Resistance sweet, delicious fight:
O night! O doubly happy night!

JOHANNES SECUNDUS

Contention obstinate succeeds;
The tender Loves contention feeds.
By that, redoubled ardour burns;
By that, redoubled strength returns.
Now o'er her neck take nimble flight,
Her breast, as spotless ivory white,
Her waist of gradual rising charms,
Soft-moulded legs, smooth-polished arms;
Search all the tracts, in curious sport,
Conductive to the Cyprian court;
Through all the dark recesses go,
And all the shady coverts know:
To this, unnumbered kisses join,
Unnumbered as the stars that shine,
Commingling rays of blended light:
O night! O doubly happy night!

Then, spare no blandishments of love:
Sounds that with softening flattery move:
Sighs that with soothing murmur please:
The injured virgin to appease:
Such, as when Zephyr fans the grove,
Or coos the amorous billing dove,
Or sings the swan with tuneful breath,
Conscious of near-approaching death:
Till, pierced by Cupid's powerful dart,
As by degrees relents her heart,
The virgin, less and less severe,
Quits by degrees her stubborn fear;
Now, on your arms her neck reclines,
Now, with your arms her neck entwines,
As love's resistless flames incite:
O night! O doubly happy night!

Part II: Medieval to Early Renaissance

Sweet kisses shall reward your pains,
Kisses which no rude rapine stains,
From lips on swelling lips that swell,
From lips on dwelling lips that dwell,
That play return with equal play,
That bliss with equal bliss repay,
That vital stores from either heart,
Imbibing, soul for soul impart;
Till now the maid, adventurous grown,
Attempts new frolics of her own;
Now suffers, strangers to the way,
Her far more daring hands to stray;
Now sports far more salacious seeks;
Now words far more licentious speaks,
Words that past sufferings well requite:
O night! O doubly happy night!

To arms! to arms! now Cupid sounds;
Now is the time for grateful wounds:
Here Venus waves the nimble spear,
Venus is warlike goddess here.
Here, not thy sister, Mars, presides;
Thy mistress in those conflicts prides.
While close engage the struggling foes,
And restless, breast to breast oppose;
While eager this disputes the field,
And that alike disdains to yield,
Till lo! in breathless transports tost,
Till, in resistless raptures lost,
Their limbs with liquid dews distil,
Their hearts with pleasing horrors thrill,
And faint away in wild delight:
O night! O doubly happy night!

O may you oft these sports renew,
And through long days and nights pursue;
With many an early moon begun,
Prolonged to many a setting sun.
May a fair offspring crown your joys,
Of prattling girls and smiling boys;
And yet another offspring rise,
Sweet objects to parental eyes,
The cares assiduous to assuage
That still solicit querulous age;
Careful your trembling limbs to stay,
That fail with unperceived decay;
Pious, when summoned hence you go,
The last kind office to bestow,
Office, with unfeigned sorrow paid:
Thrice happy youth! thrice happy maid!

* * *

YU CH'IEN, 1398-1457
English version by David Rafael Wang

The Honeymooners

Outside the city gate willows rise like smoke
At the source of West Lake water slaps into the sky
Twin oars carry along delicate wrists and a brocade skirt
And mandarin ducks gather near the lotus-gathering boat.

Part II: Medieval to Early Renaissance

T'ANG YIN, 1470-1523
English version by David Rafael Wang

Words for a Picture of Newlyweds

THIS POEM was written by T'ang Yin to accompany his scroll of painting on the same subject. T'ang Yin, nicknamed "Elder Tiger," is renowned both as poet and painter.

> Last night the cherry-apple was sprinkled with rain
> Several petals, moistened, were about to talk
> A fair lady, aroused, stepped out of her room
> Raising her mirror she compared their looks
> "Between the flowers and me, which would you
>   choose?"
> "The flower is more attractive," replied her love
> Upon hearing him, she lovingly rebuked:
> "So you prefer dead flowers to a living soul?"
> Crushing the petals she threw them at his feet
> "Tonight, go *sleep* with your flowers alone!"

PART III
Renaissance to 1900

> *But above all, away vile jealousy,*
>   *The evil of evils, just cause to be unjust;*
> *How can he love, suspecting treachery?*
> *How can she love where love cannot win trust?*

Sɪʀ Pʜɪʟɪᴘ Sɪᴅɴᴇʏ warns against jealousy and other problems, but he writes too of the joys of marriage, and he counts nuptial union as one of the glories of nature:

> *Let Mother Earth now deck herself in flowers,*
>   *To see her offspring seek a good increase ...*

Married love and sweet affection drive away the "lawless lust" of Cupid, and "war of thoughts is swallowed up in peace."

Sidney's poem, which opens the group of English poems in Part Three, is one of the hundreds of epithalamia written by Renaissance poets, and it illustrates a trend: English nuptial poets liked to give advice. Their works were highly varied, drawing on the several traditions—the Sapphic-Catullan lyric, the singing match, the rhetorical narrative, and the sensuous, allegorized *Song of Solomon*. Nuptial poetry flourished as never before, and small wonder, for it flowed from the pens of Spenser, Shakespeare, Milton, Donne, and Jonson.

Although student poems are not included here, it should be noted that the universities published large collections for every royal wedding—poems mostly in Latin, but some in Greek, Hebrew, Italian, French, Spanish, Arabic, and, after mid-seventeenth century, a few in English. In 1613, Oxford published 230 poems for the marriage of Princess Elizabeth, daughter of James I, to Frederick, Count Palatine

Part III: Renaissance to 1900

of the Rhine. In 1625, Oxford published 129 poems for Charles I and Henrietta Maria, and in 1662, more than a hundred for Charles II and Katharine. Cambridge published 91 nuptial poems for Charles I and Henrietta Maria, and 75 for Charles II and Katharine.

Many of the English nuptial lyrics were part of longer literary works—they appeared in romances, masques, plays, epics, and other narrative poems, and in devotional works. Sir Philip Sidney's epithalamium was a song in his pastoral romance, the *Arcadia*, written for his sister, the Countess of Pembroke. The poem by the young James VI of Scotland, later James I of England, came from a wedding masque which he wrote for a friend. The translation of the *Song of Solomon* is from the King James Bible, and the translation of the 45th Psalm is from the Book of Common Prayer.

Edmund Spenser's *Epithalamion* for his own marriage was published along with his sonnet sequence, the *Amoretti*. His poem on the union of rivers is from his romantic epic, *The Faerie Queene*.

Shakespeare's nuptial poems all come from his comedies, except for the epithalamium spoken by Juliet, presaging the tragedy to come:

> *Come, gentle night, come, loving, black-brow'd night,*
> *Give me my Romeo; and, when he shall die,*
> *Take him and cut him out in little stars,*
> *And he will make the face of heaven so fine*
> *That all the world will be in love with night*
> *And pay no worship to the garish sun.*

John Donne's "Epithalamion Made at Lincoln's Inn" is in some manuscripts entitled "Epithalamion on a Citizen," and this title has suggested to some readers that the poem was not written for an actual wedding but for some kind of entertainment, possibly a performance at midsummer revels when Donne was a young law student. Michael Drayton's fairy chorus, from the "Prothalamion" of *The Muses Elizium*, is reminiscent of the midsummer revels in Shakespeare's *A Midsummer Night's Dream*. The bridal customs referred to in Drayton's work are described in a chapter, "The Manner of Rejoicings at Marriages and Weddings," in George Puttenham's book, *The Arte of English Poesie*, published in 1589. He tells how the first part of the epithalamium was customarily sung as the bride and her husband were brought to their bed:

PART III: RENAISSANCE TO 1900

> *... and the tunes of the songs were very loud and shrill, to the intent there might no noise be heard out of the bedchamber by the shrieking and outcry of the young damosell feeling the first forces of her stiff and rigorous young man, she being, as all virgins, tender and weak, and unexpert in those manner of affairs. For which purpose also they used by old nurses (appointed to that service) to suppress the noise by casting of pots full of nuts round about the chamber upon the hard floor or pavement. . . .*

Ben Jonson's epithalamia come from two of his nuptial masques. Webster's dark song is from his tragedy *The Duchess of Malfi*. John Milton's epithalamium for Adam and Eve appears in Book IV of *Paradise Lost*, and extracts are given in this section. Dryden's two nuptial songs are from the plays *Amboyna* and *Marriage-à-la-Mode*. Tennyson's nuptial song appears at the end of *In Memoriam*, the elegy written for his friend Arthur Henry Hallam, who had been engaged to the poet's sister, Emily.

During the time that the nuptial poem was assuming importance as a device in longer literary works, poets also continued to write personal nuptial tributes. One of the most personal, perhaps written to mark a wedding anniversary, is that of the only woman poet in this group, Anne Bradstreet, addressed "To My Dear and Loving Husband." Born in England, Anne Bradstreet became the first lady of literature in the Massachusetts Bay Colony. Her first book of poems, *The Tenth Muse Lately Sprung Up in America*, brought to the new world some of the old world's traditions in occasional poetry.

The English poems in Part Three are followed by a miscellaneous group of European poems. Extracts have been translated from works by Marot, Ronsard, and Marino. The section ends with a group of German poems, including a lyric by Goethe and a literary ballad by Heinrich Heine, the only ballad in this anthology.

The theme *Liebe und Leid*—love inseparably connected with suffering, or love inevitably followed by suffering—is a favorite theme in German nuptial poems, as in other German literature—in medieval lyric and epic, and above all in the *Nibelungenlied* and in Gottfried von Strassburg's *Tristan und Isolde*. In the *Nibelungenlied* this theme takes the nature of a *leitmotif*, occurring for the first time in *aventiure*

Part III: Renaissance to 1900

1, 17, where Kriemhild tells her mother that she knows very well how love is followed by suffering, and that she intends to avoid both:

> "Die rede lât belîben," sprach si, "frouwe mîn.
> ez ist an manegen wîben vil dicke worden scîn
> wie liebe mit leide ze jungest lônen kan.
> ich sol si mîden beide, sone kan mir nimmer missegân."

But Kriemhild is destined for both love and suffering—her marriage to Siegfried ends when he is killed by Hagen, and her marriage to Etzel ends with the violent death of the couple amid general bloodshed and revenge. The poet concludes, in *aventiure* 39, 2378, with the remark that Kriemhild's love ended in suffering as does all love at all times:

> mit leide was verendet des küniges hôhgezît,
> als ie diu liebe leide z'aller jungeste gît.

In *Tristan und Isolde*, Gottfried explains that only the person who is ready to endure both love and pain and to accept wholeheartedly this polarity is an *anima nobilis*, an *edelez herze*. After the Middle Ages the theme continues to occur, especially in the literature of the seventeenth and nineteenth centuries and in folk songs.

Part Three concludes with two Japanese lyrics and nine *senryu*, colloquial verses which are often parodic or satiric. The ones translated here pertain to weddings and new marriage.

English

SIR PHILIP SIDNEY, 1554-1586

O Hymen, Long Their Coupled Joys Maintain!
From *The Countess of Pembroke's Arcadia* (Third Eclogues)
Song of the shepherd Dicus at the Marriage of Thyrsis and Kala

Let Mother Earth now deck herself in flowers,
   To see her offspring seek a good increase,
Where justest love doth vanquish Cupid's powers,
   And war of thoughts is swallowed up in peace,
     Which never may decrease,
     But, like the turtles fair,
     Live one in two, a well-united pair;
     Which that no charm may stain,
     O Hymen, long their coupled joys maintain!

O Heaven, awake! show forth thy stately face;
   Let not these slumb'ring clouds thy beauties hide,
But with thy cheerful presence help to grace
   The honest bridegroom and the bashful bride;
     Whose loves may ever bide,
     Like to the elm and vine,
     With mutual embracements them to twine;
     In which delightful pain,
     O Hymen, long their coupled joys maintain!

Ye Muses all, which chaste effects allow,
   And have to Thyrsis shewed your secret skill,

To this chaste love your sacred favours bow;
  And so to him and her your gifts distill,
    That they all vice may kill,
    And, like to lilies pure,
    May please all eyes, and spotless may endure;
    Where that all bliss may reign,
    O Hymen, long their coupled joys maintain!

Ye nymphs which in the waters empire have,
  Since Thyrsis' music oft doth yield you praise,
Grant to the thing which we for Thyrsis crave:
  Let one time, but long first, close up their days,
    One grave their bodies seize;
    And like two rivers sweet,
    When they, though divers, do together meet,
    One stream both streams contain:
    O Hymen, long their coupled joys maintain!

Pan, Father Pan, the god of silly sheep,
  Whose care is cause that they in number grow,
Have much more care of them that them do keep,
  Since from these good the others' good doth flow,
    And make their issue show
    In number like the herd
    Of younglings, which thyself with love hast reared;
    Or like the drops of rain:
    O Hymen, long their coupled joys maintain!

Virtue, if not a god, yet God's chief part,
  Be thou the knot of this their open vow,
That still he be her head, she be his heart,
  He lean to her, she unto him do bow,
    Each other still allow;
    Like oak and mistletoe,
    Her strength from him, his praise from her do grow:

In which most lovely train,
　　　O Hymen, long their coupled joys maintain!

But thou, foul Cupid, sire to lawless lust,
　　Be thou far hence with thy empoisoned dart,
Which, though of glittering gold, shall here take rust,
　　Where simple love, which chasteness doth impart,
　　　Avoids thy hurtful art;
　　　Not needing charming skill,
　　　Such minds with sweet affections for to fill;
　　　Which being pure and plain,
　　　O Hymen, long their coupled joys maintain!

All churlish words, shrewd answers, crabbed looks,
　　All privateness, self-seeking, inward spite,
All waywardness, which nothing kindly brooks,
　　All strife for toys and claiming master's right,
　　　Be hence, aye put to flight;
　　　All stirring husband's hate
　　　'Gainst neighbour's good for womanish debate,
　　　Be fled, as things most vain:
　　　O Hymen, long their coupled joys maintain!

All peacock pride, and fruits of peacock's pride,
　　Longing to be with loss of substance gay;
With retchlessness what may the house betide,
　　So that you may on higher slippers stay,
　　　For ever hence away:
　　　Yet let not sluttery,
　　　The sink of filth, be counted housewifery;
　　　But keeping wholesome mean,
　　　O Hymen, long their coupled joys maintain!

But above all, away vile jealousy,
　　The evil of evils, just cause to be unjust;

How can he love, suspecting treachery?
How can she love where love cannot win trust?
Go, snake, hide thee in dust,
Ne dare once shew thy face
Where open hearts do hold so constant place,
That they thy sting restrain:
O Hymen, long their coupled joys maintain!

The earth is decked with flowers, the heavens displayed,
Muses grant gifts, Nymphs long and joined life,
Pan store of babes, Virtue their thoughts well stayed,
Cupid's lust gone, and gone is bitter strife.
Happy man, happy wife!
No pride shall them oppress,
Nor yet shall yield to loathsome sluttishness,
And jealousy is slain;
For Hymen will their coupled joys maintain.

* * *

JAMES VI OF SCOTLAND, 1566-1625

An Epithalamion upon the Marquis of Huntilies Marriage

THE NUPTIAL POEM written by the young king (later James I of England) concentrates on the prospective offspring of the bridal couple. James wishes that the couple may become "broodie"—inclined to breed—so that a child will soon arrive. He asks for blessings from an assortment of seventeen Roman gods, all obscure except Venus and Hymen. Among them are Volumnia, the Well-Wisher, tutelary deity of new-born infants; Vitumnus, who gives vital breath to babies; Sentinus, who bestows the power of sensation; Prorsa, who presides over birth with the head foremost; Egeria, a Roman goddess of fountains worshiped as a goddess of childbirth; Lucina, goddess of childbirth who brings the child to light; Levana, who presides over the father's lifting up the child as a sign of acknowledgment; Vaticanus, who presides over the child's first cry; Cunina, guardian of the cradle; Rumina, protectress of infants at the breast; Educa, who presides over the child's eating; Potina, who supervises the child's drinking; Statilinus, who protects the baby on his first attempt at standing alone; and Fortune, the god of chance.

If ever I o mighty Gods have done you service true
In setting forth by painful pen your glorious praises due

If on the forked hill I tread, if ever I did press
To drink of the Pegasian spring, that flows without release

If ever I on Pindus dwelled, and from that sacred hill
The ears of every living thing did with your fame fulfill

Which by the trumpet of my verse I made for to resound
From pole to pole through every where of this immobile round

Then grant to me who patron am of Hymen's triumph here
That all your graces may upon this Hymen's band appear.

O son of Cytherea fair, and thou Thalasse withall
Grant that this band may happily to these coupled folks befall

And o Volumna print a will into their coupled hearts
Which may retain that union aye, on either of their parts

O Venus make them broodie als for to produce with speed
Wherein they may revive again a blest and happy seed

Vitumnus and Sentinus als in happy time indue
The child whenas it is conceived, with life and senses true

O Prosa with Egeria joined, and thou Lucina bright
Her dolours make into her birth, by your assisting light;

O thou Levana do with love and carefulness embrace
The babe when it is born which should extend their
    happy race

O Vagitanus play thy part and safely do it keep
From all misfortunes and mischance whenas it first does weep

O thou Cunina carefully do watch the cradle aye
Preserving it from sickness or from harm in any way

Rumina, with Edusa, and Potina joined, do see
That when it sucking is or weaned, the food may wholesome be

And also for their upbringing o Statilinus care
That to their perfect age it may a happy way prepare

And thou o Fortune to conclude, make these and all their race
To be beloved by Gods and men, and thrive in every case.

If for my sake ye Gods above these graces will bestow
Before these nuptial days some sign to me for promise show.

* * *

From THE BOOK OF COMMON PRAYER

Psalm 45, Eructavit cor meum

LOOKING AT the *Eructavit cor meum* as a poem for a human marriage, one sees in it praise of the bridegroom, the bride, their apparel and gifts, and the children they will have. In the opening lines, the poet tells of his eagerness to sing a tribute to the King who is the bridegroom, and in the closing lines he promises that his poem will make the King's name immortal. Through his art, the wedding poet is paying the greatest possible tribute.

The notion of human marriage allegorized as a spiritual marriage runs through Christian poetry. Psalm 45 from the Psalter in the Book of Common Prayer (Psalm 44 of the Vulgate) was thus allegorically interpreted by Christian commentators.

> My heart overfloweth with a good matter; I speak the things which I have made concerning the King. My tongue is the pen of a ready writer.
>
> Thou art fairer than the children of men; full of grace are thy lips, because God hath blessed thee for ever.
>
> Gird thee with thy sword upon thy thigh, O thou Most Mighty, according to thy worship and renown.
>
> Good luck have thou with thine honour: ride on, because of the word of truth, of meekness, and righteousness; and thy right hand shall teach thee terrible things.
>
> Thy arrows are very sharp in the heart of the King's enemies, and the people shall be subdued unto thee.
>
> Thy seat, O God, endureth for ever; the sceptre of thy kingdom is a right sceptre.
>
> Thou hast loved righteousness, and hated iniquity; wherefore God, even thy God, hath anointed thee with the oil of gladness above thy fellows.
>
> All thy garments smell of myrrh, aloes, and cassia; out of the ivory palaces, whereby they have made thee glad.
>
> Kings' daughters are among thy honourable women; upon thy right hand doth stand the queen in a vesture of gold, wrought about with divers colours.

Part III: Renaissance to 1900

Hearken, O daughter, and consider; incline thine ear; forget also thine own people, and thy father's house.

So shall the King have pleasure in thy beauty; for he is thy Lord, and worship thou him.

And the daughter of Tyre shall be there with a gift; like as the rich also among the people shall make their supplication before thee.

The King's daughter is all glorious within; her clothing is of wrought gold.

She shall be brought unto the King in raiment of needlework: the virgins that be her fellows shall bear her company, and shall be brought unto thee.

With joy and gladness shall they be brought, and shall enter into the King's palace.

Instead of thy fathers, thou shalt have children, whom thou mayest make princes in all lands.

I will make thy Name to be remembered from one generation to another; therefore shall the people give thanks unto thee, world without end.

* * *

From THE HOLY BIBLE
Authorized King James Version

The Song of Solomon

LIKE THE PAGAN nuptial poem, the Canticle ascribed to Solomon may owe something of its language and structure to the fertility rituals that celebrate the mystical union of Heaven and Earth and the sowing of seed, enabling the earth, watered by the rain, to produce new life.

Christian commentators wrote that it was Solomon who composed the first epithalamium, often referred to as "the sacred pastoral," but that David also knew the art. The commentators explained that the Hebrews passed the art to the Greeks. Writers as early as Origen, c. 185-284, considered the Canticle to be an epic in the form of a drama celebrating the Incarnation: the wedding of Christ, the bridegroom, to the flesh, the bride, in the marriage chamber of the Virgin Mary. Origen thought the dialogue to be among four participants: the bride and the bridegroom and two choruses—one chorus composed of companions of the bridegroom (angels and saints) and the other of companions of the bride (the faithful of the Church on earth). St. Augustine was another who viewed the Canticle as a metaphorical poem of rejoicing over the mystical marriage of Christ and the Church. The Catholic allegorical view of the Canticle was adhered to on the whole by the Reformed Church.

Although modern scholars interpret the Canticle in various ways, many agree that at its origin it probably concerned a wedding or union of human lovers, that it is a literary rather than a folk pastoral, it is erotic, and it displays many parallels with other wedding literature. The Song of Solomon has echoed for many centuries in the poetry of devotion, love, and marriage.

CHAPTER I

The song of songs, which *is* Solomon's.

Let him kiss me with the kisses of his mouth: for thy love *is* better than wine.

Because of the savour of thy good ointments thy name *is as* ointment poured forth, therefore do the virgins love thee.

Draw me, we will run after thee: the king hath brought me into his chambers: we will be glad and rejoice in thee, we will remember thy love more than wine: the upright love thee.

I *am* black, but comely, O ye daughters of Jerusalem, as the tents of Kedar, as the curtains of Solomon.

Look not upon me, because I *am* black, because the sun hath looked upon me: my mother's children were angry with me; they made me the keeper of the vineyards; *but* mine own vineyard have I not kept.

Tell me, O thou whom my soul loveth, where thou feedest, where thou makest *thy flock* to rest at noon: for why should I be as one that turneth aside by the flocks of thy companions?

If thou know not, O thou fairest among women, go thy way forth by the footsteps of the flock, and feed thy kids beside the shepherds' tents.

I have compared thee, O my love, to a company of horses in Pharaoh's chariots.

Thy cheeks are comely with rows *of jewels*, thy neck with chains *of gold*.

We will make thee borders of gold with studs of silver.

While the king *sitteth* at his table, my spikenard sendeth forth the smell thereof.

A bundle of myrrh *is* my well-beloved unto me; he shall lie all night betwixt my breasts.

My beloved *is* unto me *as* a cluster of camphire in the vineyards of En-gedi.

Behold, thou *art* fair, my love; behold, thou *art* fair; thou *hast* doves' eyes.

Behold, thou *art* fair, my beloved, yea, pleasant: also our bed *is* green.

The beams of our house *are* cedar, *and* our rafters of fir.

CHAPTER 2

I *AM* the rose of Sharon, *and* the lily of the valleys.

As the lily among thorns, so *is* my love among the daughters.

As the apple tree among the trees of the wood, so *is*

my beloved among the sons. I sat down under his shadow with great delight, and his fruit *was* sweet to my taste.

He brought me to the banqueting house, and his banner over me *was* love.

Stay me with flagons, comfort me with apples: for I *am* sick of love.

His left hand *is* under my head, and his right hand doth embrace me.

I charge you, O ye daughters of Jerusalem, by the roes, and by the hinds of the field, that ye stir not up, nor awake *my* love, till he please.

The voice of my beloved! behold, he cometh leaping upon the mountains, skipping upon the hills.

My beloved is like a roe or a young hart: behold, he standeth behind our wall, he looketh forth at the windows, shewing himself through the lattice.

My beloved spake, and said unto me, Rise up, my love, my fair one, and come away.

For, lo, the winter is past, the rain is over *and* gone;

The flowers appear on the earth; the time of the singing *of birds* is come, and the voice of the turtle is heard in our land;

The fig tree putteth forth her green figs, and the vines *with* the tender grape give a *good* smell. Arise, my love, my fair one, and come away.

O my dove, *that art* in the clefts of the rock, in the secret *places* of the stairs, let me see thy countenance, let me hear thy voice; for sweet *is* thy voice, and thy countenance *is* comely.

Take us the foxes, the little foxes, that spoil the vines: for our vines *have* tender grapes.

My beloved *is* mine, and I *am* his: he feedeth among the lilies.

Until the day break, and the shadows flee away,

turn, my beloved, and be thou like a roe or a young hart upon the mountains of Bether.

CHAPTER 3

By night on my bed I sought him whom my soul loveth: I sought him, but I found him not.

I will rise now, and go about the city in the streets, and in the broad ways I will seek him whom my soul loveth: I sought him, but I found him not.

The watchmen that go about the city found me: *to whom I said*, Saw ye him whom my soul loveth?

It was but a little that I passed from them, but I found him whom my soul loveth: I held him, and would not let him go, until I had brought him into my mother's house, and into the chamber of her that conceived me.

I charge you, O ye daughters of Jerusalem, by the roes, and by the hinds of the field, that ye stir not up, nor awake *my* love, till he please.

Who *is* this that cometh out of the wilderness like pillars of smoke, perfumed with myrrh and frankincense, with all powders of the merchant?

Behold his bed, which *is* Solomon's; threescore valiant men *are* about it, of the valiant of Israel.

They all hold swords, *being* expert in war: every man *hath* his sword upon his thigh because of fear in the night.

King Solomon made himself a chariot of the wood of Lebanon.

He made the pillars thereof *of* silver, the bottom thereof *of* gold, the covering of it *of* purple, the midst thereof being paved *with* love, for the daughters of Jerusalem.

Go forth, O ye daughters of Zion, and behold king

Solomon with the crown wherewith his mother crowned him in the day of his espousals, and in the day of the gladness of his heart.

CHAPTER 4

Behold, thou *art* fair, my love; behold, thou *art* fair; thou *hast* doves' eyes within thy locks: thy hair *is* as a flock of goats, that appear from mount Gilead.

Thy teeth *are* like a flock *of sheep that are even* shorn, which came up from the washing; whereof every one bear twins, and none *is* barren among them.

Thy lips *are* like a thread of scarlet, and thy speech *is* comely: thy temples *are* like a piece of a pomegranate within thy locks.

Thy neck *is* like the tower of David builded for an armoury, whereon there hang a thousand bucklers, all shields of mighty men.

Thy two breasts *are* like two young roes that are twins, which feed among the lilies.

Until the day break, and the shadows flee away, I will get me to the mountain of myrrh, and to the hill of frankincense.

Thou *art* all fair, my love; *there is* no spot in thee.

Come with me from Lebanon, *my* spouse, with me from Lebanon: look from the top of Amana, from the top of Shenir and Hermon, from the lions' dens, from the mountains of the leopards.

Thou hast ravished my heart, my sister, *my* spouse; thou hast ravished my heart with one of thine eyes, with one chain of thy neck.

How fair is thy love, my sister, *my* spouse! how much better is thy love than wine! and the smell of thine ointments than all spices!

Thy lips, O *my* spouse, drop *as* the honeycomb:

Part III: Renaissance to 1900

honey and milk *are* under thy tongue; and the smell of thy garments *is* like the smell of Lebanon.

A garden inclosed *is* my sister, *my* spouse; a spring shut up, a fountain sealed.

Thy plants *are* an orchard of pomegranates, with pleasant fruits; camphire, with spikenard,

Spikenard and saffron; calamus and cinnamon, with all trees of frankincense; myrrh and aloes, with all the chief spices:

A fountain of gardens, a well of living waters, and streams from Lebanon.

Awake, O north wind; and come, thou south; blow upon my garden, *that* the spices thereof may flow out. Let my beloved come into his garden, and eat his pleasant fruits. . . .

* * *

EDMUND SPENSER, 1552-1599

Epithalamion

EDMUND SPENSER's great poem for his own wedding, is an almost chronological account of the events of the wedding day, with the bridegroom himself serving as master of ceremonies of the joyous celebration involving man, nature, pagan deities and creatures of myth, and culminating in Christian ritual and prayer for immortality.

It has been suggested by A. Kent Hieatt that the twenty-four stanzas of the poem represent the twenty-four hours of the wedding day, and that the change in the refrain in Stanza 17, "The woods *no* more shall answer, nor your echo ring," represents the time when daylight changes to darkness in the Irish countryside where the wedding takes place. During the daylight hours, the woods echo the sounds of the celebration; at night, quiet comes, and the woods no longer echo.

Apparently the couple chose as their wedding date the longest day of the year, and the bridegroom wryly comments that it was a mistake:

> *To choose the longest day in all the year,*
> *And shortest night, when longest fitter were . . .*

In keeping with the ancient custom of including a *fescennine* or bawdy passage in an epithalamium, Spenser remarks that his own wedding night may be "Like as when Jove with fair Alcmena lay." Spenser's contemporaries, more familiar with myth than most twentieth-century readers are, would have laughed knowingly: Jove, the god who made a habit of assuming various shapes and coming to earth to seduce mortal maidens, disguised himself as Alcmena's husband and, "her pleasures longer to partake," commanded the sun to stand still, extending the love-making to "three nights in one."

Spenser's poem opens with the bridegroom calling on the Muses.

> Ye learned sisters which have oftentimes
> Been to me aiding, others to adorn,
> Whom ye thought worthy of your graceful rhymes,
> That even the greatest did not greatly scorn
> To hear their names sung in your simple lays,
> But joyed in their praise;
> And when ye list your own mishaps to mourn,
> Which death, or love, or fortune's wreck did raise,
> Your string could soon to sadder tenor turn,
> And teach the woods and waters to lament
> Your doleful dreriment:
> Now lay those sorrowful complaints aside;
> And, having all your heads with garlands crowned,
> Help me mine own love's praises to resound;
> Ne let the same of any be envied:
> So Orpheus did for his own bride!
> So I unto myself alone will sing;
> The woods shall to me answer, and my echo ring.

Early, before the world's light-giving lamp
His golden beam upon the hills doth spread,
Having dispersed the night's uncheerful damp,
Do ye awake; and, with fresh lusty-hed,
Go to the bower of my belovéd love,
My truest turtle dove;
Bid her awake; for Hymen is awake,
And long since ready forth his mask to move,
With his bright tead that flames with many a flake,
And many a bachelor to wait on him,
In their fresh garments trim.
Bid her awake therefore, and soon her dight,
For lo! the wishéd day is come at last,
That shall, for all the pains and sorrows past,
Pay to her usury of long delight:
And, whilst she doth her dight,
Do ye to her of joy and solace sing,
That all the woods may answer, and your echo ring.

Bring with you all the nymphs that you can hear
Both of the rivers and the forests green,
And of the sea that neighbours to her near,
All with gay garlands goodly well beseen.
And let them also with them bring in hand
Another gay garland,
For my fair love, of lilies and of roses,
Bound true-love wise with a blue silk riband.
And let them make great store of bridal posies,
And let them eke bring store of other flowers,
To deck the bridal bowers.
And let the ground whereas her foot shall tread,
For fear the stones her tender foot should wrong,
Be strewed with fragrant flowers all along,
And diapered like the discoloured mead.
Which done, do at her chamber door await,

For she will waken straight;
The whiles do ye this song unto her sing,
The woods shall to you answer, and your echo ring.

Ye nymphs of Mulla, which with careful heed
The silver scaly trouts do tend full well,
And greedy pikes which use therein to feed,
(Those trouts and pikes all others do excel);
And ye likewise, which keep the rushy lake,
Where none do fishes take;
Bind up the locks the which hang scattered light,
And in his waters, which your mirror make,
Behold your faces as the crystal bright,
That when you come whereas my love doth lie,
No blemish she may spie.
And eke, ye light-foot maids, which keep the deer
That on the hoary mountain use to tower;
And the wild wolves, which seek them to devour,
With your steel darts do chase from coming near;
Be also present here,
To help to deck her, and to help to sing,
That all the woods may answer, and your echo ring.

Wake now, my love, awake! for it is time;
The rosy Morn long since left Tithon's bed,
All ready to her silver coach to climb;
And Phoebus 'gins to show his glorious head.
Hark! how the cheerful birds do chant their lays
And carol of Love's praise.
The merry lark her matins sings aloft;
The thrush replies; the mavis descant plays;
The ouzel shrills; the ruddock warbles soft:
So goodly all agree, with sweet consent,
To this day's merriment.
Ah! my dear love, why do you sleep thus long,

When meeter were that ye should now awake,
T' await the coming of your joyous make,
And hearken to the birds' love-learned song,
The dewy leaves among!
For they of joy and pleasance to you sing,
That all the woods them answer, and their echo ring.

My love is now awake out of her dream,
And her fair eyes, like stars that dimmed wére
With darksome cloud, now shew their goodly beams
More bright than Hesperus his head doth rear.
Come now, ye damsels, daughters of delight,
Help quickly her to dight:
But first come ye, fair Hours, which were begot
In Jove's sweet paradise of day and night,
Which do the seasons of the year allot,
And all that ever in this world is fair
Do make and still repair:
And ye three handmaids of the Cyprian queen,
The which do still adorn her beauty's pride,
Help to adorn my beautifullest bride:
And, as ye her array, still throw between
Some graces to be seen;
And, as ye use to Venus, to her sing,
The whiles the woods shall answer, and your echo ring.

Now is my love all ready forth to come:
Let all the virgins therefore well await:
And ye fresh boys, that tend upon her groom,
Prepare yourselves, for he is coming straight.
Set all your things in seemly good array,
Fit for so joyful day,
The joyful'st day that ever sun did see.
Fair sun! show forth thy favourable ray,
And let thy lifull heat not fervent be,

For fear of burning her sunshiny face,
Her beauty to disgrace.
O fairest Phoebus! father of the Muse!
If ever I did honour thee aright,
Or sing the thing that mote thy mind delight,
Do not thy servant's simple boon refuse;
But let this day, let this one day be mine;
Let all the rest be thine.
Then I thy sovereign praises loud will sing,
That all the woods shall answer, and their echo ring.

Hark! how the minstrels 'gin to shrill aloud
Their merry music that resounds from far,
The pipe, the tabor, and the trembling croud,
That well agree withouten breach or jar.
But most of all, the damsels do delight
When they their timbrels smite,
And thereunto do dance and carol sweet,
That all the senses they do ravish quite;
The whiles the boys run up and down the street,
Crying aloud with strong confuséd noise,
As if it were one voice,
Hymen! Io Hymen! Hymen! they do shout;
That even to the heavens their shouting shrill
Doth reach, and all the firmament doth fill:
To which the people standing all about,
As in approvance, do thereto applaud,
And loud advance her laud;
And evermore they Hymen, Hymen, sing,
That all the woods them answer, and their echo ring.

Lo! where she comes along with portly pace,
Like Phoebe, from her chamber of the East,
Arising forth to run her mighty race;

Clad all in white, that seems a virgin best.
So well it her beseems, that ye would ween
Some angel she had been.
Her long loose yellow locks like golden wire,
Sprinkled with pearl and pearling flowers atween,
Do like a golden mantle her attire,
And, being crownéd with a garland green,
Seem like some maiden queen.
Her modest eyes, abashéd to behold
So many gazers as on her do stare,
Upon the lowly ground affixéd are;
Ne dare lift up her countenance too bold,
But blush to hear her praises sung so loud,
So far from being proud.
Natheless do ye still loud her praises sing,
That all the woods may answer, and your echo ring.

Tell me, ye merchants' daughters, did ye see
So fair a creature in your town before;
So sweet, so lovely, and so mild as she,
Adorned with beauty's grace and virtue's store?
Her goodly eyes like sapphires shining bright,
Her forehead ivory white,
Her cheeks like apples which the sun hath rudded,
Her lips like cherries charming men to bite,
Her breast like to a bowl of cream uncrudded,
Her paps like lilies budded,
Her snowy neck like to a marble tower;
And all her body like a palace fair,
Ascending up, with many a stately stair,
To honour's seat and chastity's sweet bower.
Why stand ye still, ye virgins, in amaze,
Upon her so to gaze,
Whiles ye forget your former lay to sing,
To which the woods did answer, and your echo ring?

But if ye saw that which no eyes can see,
The inward beauty of her lively sprite,
Garnished with heavenly gifts of high degree,
Much more then would ye wonder at that sight,
And stand astonished like to those which read
Medusa's mazeful head.
There dwells sweet love, and constant chastity
Unspotted faith, and comely womanhood,
Regard of honour, and mild modesty;
There virtue reigns as queen in royal throne
And giveth laws alone,
The which the base affections do obey,
And yield their services unto her will;
Ne thought of thing uncomely ever may
Thereto approach to tempt her mind to ill.
Had ye once seen these her celestial treasures,
And unrevealéd pleasures,
Then would ye wonder, and her praises sing,
That all the woods should answer, and your echo ring.

Open the temple gates unto my love,
Open them wide that she may enter in;
And all the posts adorn as doth behove,
And all the pillars deck with garlands trim,
For to receive this saint with honour due,
That cometh in to you.
With trembling steps and humble reverence
She cometh in, before th' Almighty's view;
Of her ye virgins learn obedience,
When so ye come into those holy places,
To humble your proud faces.
Bring her up to th' high altar, that she may
The sacred ceremonies there partake,
The which do endless matrimony make;
And let the roaring organs loudly play
The praises of the Lord in lively notes;

The whiles, with hollow throats,
The choristers the joyous anthem sing,
That all the woods may answer, and their echo ring.

Behold, whiles she before the altar stands,
Hearing the holy priest that to her speaks,
And blesseth her with his two happy hands,
How the red roses flush up in her cheeks,
And the pure snow, with goodly vermeil stain,
Like crimson died in grain:
That even th' angels which continually
About the sacred altar do remain,
Forget their service and about her fly,
Oft peeping in her face, that seems more fair,
The more they on it stare.
But her sad eyes, still fastened on the ground,
Are governéd with goodly modesty,
That suffers not one look to glance awry,
Which may let in a little thought unsound.
Why blush ye, love, to give to me your hand,
The pledge of all our band!
Sing, ye sweet angels, "Alleluia" sing,
That all the woods may answer, and your echo ring.

Now all is done: bring home the bride again;
Bring home the triumph of our victory:
Bring home with you the glory of her gain,
With joyance bring her and with jollity.
Never had man more joyful day than this,
Whom Heaven would heap with bliss;
Make feast therefore now all this livelong day;
This day for ever to me holy is.
Pour out the wine without restraint or stay,
Pour not by cups, but by the belly-full,

Pour out to all that wull,
And sprinkle all the posts and walls with wine,
That they may sweat and drunken be withal.
Crown ye God Bacchus with a coronal,
And Hymen also crown with wreaths of vine;
And let the Graces dance unto the rest,
For they can do it best:
The whiles the maidens do their carol sing,
To which the woods shall answer, and their echo ring.

Ring ye the bells, ye young men of the town,
And leave your wonted labours for this day:
This day is holy; do ye write it down,
That ye for ever it remember may.
This day the sun is in his chiefest height,
With Barnaby the bright;
From whence declining daily by degrees,
He somewhat loseth of his heat and light,
When once the Crab behind his back he sees.
But for this time it ill ordainéd was,
To choose the longest day in all the year,
And shortest night, when longest fitter were:
Yet never day so long, but late would pass.
Ring ye the bells, to make it wear away,
And bonfires make all day;
And dance about them, and about them sing,
That all the woods may answer, and your echo ring.

Ah! when will this long weary day have end,
And lend me leave to come unto my love?
How slowly do the hours their numbers spend!
How slowly does sad Time his feathers move!
Haste thee, O fairest planet, to thy home,
Within the western foam:
Thy tired steeds long since have need of rest.

Long though it be, at last I see it gloom,
And the bright evening-star with golden crest,
Appear out of the East.
Fair child of beauty! glorious lamp of love!
That all the host of heaven in ranks dost lead,
And guidest lovers through the night's sad dread,
How cheerfully thou lookest from above,
And seem'st to laugh atween thy twinkling light!
As joying in the sight
Of these glad many, which for joy do sing,
That all the woods them answer, and their echo ring.

Now cease, ye damsels, your delights forepast;
Enough it is that all the day was yours:
Now day is done, and night is nighing fast,
Now bring the bride into the bridal bowers.
The night is come, now soon her disarray,
And in her bed her lay;
Lay her in lilies and in violets,
And silken curtains over her display,
And odoured sheets, and Arras coverlets.
Behold how goodly my fair love does lie,
In proud humility!
Like unto Maia, when as Jove her took
In Tempe, lying on the flowery grass,
'Twixt sleep and wake, after she weary was
With bathing in the Acidalian brook.
Now it is night, ye damsels may be gone,
And leave my love alone;
And leave likewise your former lay to sing:
The woods no more shall answer, nor your echo ring.

Now welcome, night! thou night so long expected,
That long day's labour dost at last defray,
And all my cares, which cruel Love collected,
Hast summed in one, and cancellèd for aye:

EDMUND SPENSER

Spread thy broad wing over my love and me,
That no man may us see;
And in thy sable mantle us enwrap,
From fear of peril and foul horror free.
Let no false treason seek us to entrap,
Nor any dread disquiet once annoy
The safety of our joy;
But let the night be calm, and quietsome,
Without tempestuous storms or sad affray,
Like as when Jove with fair Alcmena lay,
When he begot the great Tyrinthian groom:
Or like as when he with thyself did lie
And begot majesty.
And let the maids and young men cease to sing,
Ne let the woods them answer, nor their echo ring.

Let no lamenting cries, nor doleful tears,
Be heard all night within, nor yet without;
Ne let false whispers, breeding hidden fears,
Break gentle sleep with misconceivéd doubt.
Let no deluding dreams, nor dreadful sights,
Make sudden sad affrights;
Ne let house-fires, nor lightning's helpless harms,
Ne let the Puck, nor other evil sprites,
Ne let mischievous witches with their charms,
Ne let hobgoblins, names whose sense we see not,
Fray us with things that be not:
Let not the shriek-owl nor the stork be heard,
Nor the night raven, that still deadly yells,
Nor damnéd ghosts, called up with mighty spells,
Nor grisly vultures, make us once affeared:
Ne let th' unpleasant quire of frogs still croaking
Make us to wish their choking.
Let none of these their dreary accents sing,
Ne let the woods them answer, nor their echo ring.

But let still Silence true night-watches keep.
That sacred Peace may in assurance reign,
And timely Sleep, when it is time to sleep,
May pour his limbs forth on your pleasant plain;
The whiles an hundred little wingéd Loves,
Like divers feathered doves,
Shall fly and flutter round about your bed;
And in the secret dark that none reproves,
Their pretty stealths shall work, and snares shall spread
To filch away sweet snatches of delight,
Concealed through covert night.
Ye sons of Venus, play your sports at will!
For greedy pleasure, careless of your toys,
Thinks more upon her paradise of joys,
Than what ye do, albe it good or ill.
All night therefore attend your merry play,
For it will soon be day:
Now none doth hinder you, that say or sing,
Ne will the woods now answer, nor your echo ring.

Who is the same, which at my window peeps?
Or whose is that fair face that shines so bright?
Is it not Cynthia, she that never sleeps,
But walks about high heaven all the night?
O fairest Goddess! do thou not envy
My love with me to spy:
For thou likewise didst love, though now unthought,
And for a fleece of wool, which privily
The Latmian shepherd once unto thee brought,
His pleasures with thee wrought.
Therefore to us be favourable now;
And sith of women's labours thou hast charge,
And generation goodly dost enlarge,
Incline thy wish t' effect our wishful vow,
And the chaste womb inform with timely seed,

EDMUND SPENSER

That may our comfort breed:
Till which we cease our hopeful hap to sing;
Ne let the woods us answer, nor our echo ring.

And thou, great Juno! which with awful might
The laws of wedlock still dost patronize;
And the religion of the faith first plight,
With sacred rites hast taught to solemnize;
And eke for comfort often called art
Of women in their smart;
Eternally bind thou this lovely band,
And all thy blessings unto us impart.
And thou, glad Genius! in whose gentle hand
The bridal bower and genial bed remain,
Without blemish or stain;
And the sweet pleasure of their love's delight
With secret aid dost succour and supply,
Till they bring forth the fruitfull progeny;
Send us the timely fruit of this same night.
And thou, fair Hebe! and thou, Hymen free!
Grant that it may so be.
Till which we cease your further praise to sing:
Ne any woods shall answer, nor your echo ring.

And ye, high heavens, the temple of the gods,
In which a thousand torches flaming bright
Do burn, that to us wretched earthly clods
In dreadful darkness lend desired light;
And all ye powers which in the same remain,
More than we men can feign;
Pour out your blessing on us plenteously,
And happy influence upon us rain,
That we may raise a large posterity.
Which from the earth, which they may long possess
With lasting happiness,

(115)

Up to your haughty palaces may mount;
And, for the guerdon of their glorious merit,
May heavenly tabernacles there inherit,
Of blessed saints for to increase the count.
So let us rest, sweet love, in hope of this,
And cease till then our timely joys to sing:
The woods no more us answer, nor our echo ring!

Song! made in lieu of many ornaments,
With which my love should duly have been dect;
Which cutting off through hasty accidents,
Ye would not stay your due time to expect,
But promised both to recompense;
Be unto her a goodly ornament,
And for short time an endless monument.

Prothalamion; or A Spousal Verse, made by Edm. Spenser

In honour of the double marriage of the two honourable and virtuous ladies, the Lady Elizabeth, and the Lady Katherine Somerset, daughters to the Right Honourable the Earl of Worcester, and espoused to the two worthy gentlemen M. Henry Gilford, and M. William Peter, Esquires.

THIS IS A BETROTHAL poem, and for it Spenser apparently coined the title to indicate a song that preceded the nuptials. The "Prothalamion," Spenser's last published work, has one of the most beautiful refrains in all of English literature: "Sweet Thames! run softly, till I end my song." The line reflects the poet's life-long interest in rivers and his association of them with the tradition of nuptial poetry. This poem celebrates two weddings. To represent the two sisters who were brides, Spenser chose the pair of swans who draw the car of Venus through the sky and on her journeys by river and sea. In Spenser's time, real swans lived on the river Thames; in fact, the swans were royal property, and Queen Elizabeth employed a royal swan-herd.

EDMUND SPENSER

Calm was the day, and through the trembling air
Sweet-breathing Zephyrus did softly play
A gentle spirit, that lightly did delay
Hot Titan's beams, which then did glister fair;
When I (whom sullen care,
Through discontent of my long fruitless stay
In prince's court, and expectation vain
Of idle hopes, which still do fly away
Like empty shadows, did afflict my brain),
Walked forth to ease my pain
Along the shore of silver streaming Thames;
Whose rutty bank, the which his river hems,
Was painted all with variable flowers,
And all the meads adorned with dainty gems
Fit to deck maidens' bowers,
And crown their paramours
Against the bridal day, which is not long:
Sweet Thames! run softly, till I end my song.

There in a meadow by the river's side,
A flock of nymphs I chanced to espy,
All lovely daughters of the flood thereby,
With goodly greenish locks, all loose untied,
As each had been a bride;
And each one had a little wicker basket,
Made of fine twigs, entrailéd curiously,
In which they gathered flowers to fill their flasket,
And with fine fingers cropped full feateously
The tender stalks on high.
Of every sort which in that meadow grew,
They gathered some; the violet pallid blue,
The little daisy that at evening closes,
The virgin lily, and the primrose true,
With store of vermeil roses,
To deck their bridegroom's posies

Against the bridal day, which was not long:
Sweet Thames! run softly, till I end my song.

With that I saw two swans of goodly hue
Come softly swimming down along the Lea;
Two fairer birds I yet did never see;
The snow, which doth the top of Pindus strew,
Did never whiter shew,
Nor Jove himself, when he a swan would be
For love of Leda, whiter did appear;
Yet Leda was (they say) as white as he,
Yet not so white as these, nor nothing near;
So purely white they were
That even the gentle stream, the which them bare,
Seemed foul to them, and bade his billows spare
To wet their silken feathers, lest they might
Soil their fair plumes with water not so fair,
And mar their beauties bright,
That shone as heaven's light,
Against their bridal day, which was not long:
Sweet Thames! run softly, till I end my song.

Eftsoons the nymphs, which now had flowers their fill,
Ran all in haste to see that silver brood,
As they came floating on the crystal flood;
Whom when they saw, they stood amazéd still,
Their wond'ring eyes to fill;
Them seemed they never saw a sight so fair,
Of fowls so lovely, that they sure did deem
Them heavenly born, or to be that same pair
Which through the sky draw Venus' silver teem;
For sure they did not seem
To be begot of any earthly seed,
But rather angels, or of angels' breed;
Yet were they bred of summer's-heat, they say,

EDMUND SPENSER

In sweetest season, when each flower and weed
The earth did fresh array;
So fresh they seemed as day,
Even as their bridal day, which was not long:
Sweet Thames! run softly, till I end my song.

Then forth they all out of their baskets drew
Great store of flowers, the honour of the field,
That to the sense did fragrant odours yield;
All which upon those goodly birds they threw,
And all the waves did strew,
That like old Peneus' waters they did seem,
When down along by pleasant Tempe's shore,
Scattered with flowers, through Thessaly they stream,
That they appear, through lilies' plenteous store,
Like a bride's chamber floor.
Two of those nymphs, meanwhile, two garlands bound
Of freshest flowers which in that mead they found,
The which presenting all in trim array,
Their snowy foreheads therewithal they crowned,
Whilst one did sing this lay,
Prepared against that day,
Against their bridal day, which was not long:
Sweet Thames! run softly, till I end my song.

"Ye gentle birds! the world's fair ornament,
And heaven's glory, whom this happy hour
Doth lead unto your lovers' blissful bower,
Joy may you have, and gentle heart's content
Of your love's couplement;
And let fair Venus, that is queen of love,
With her heart-quelling son upon you smile,
Whose smile, they say, hath virtue to remove
All love's dislike, and friendship's faulty guile
For ever to assoil.

Let endless peace your steadfast hearts accord,
And blessed plenty wait upon your board;
And let your bed with pleasures chaste abound,
That fruitful issue may to you afford,
Which may your foes confound,
And make your joys redound
Upon your bridal day, which is not long:
Sweet Thames! run softly, till I end my song."

So ended she; and all the rest around
To her redoubled that her undersong,
Which said their bridal day should not be long;
And gentle echo from the neighbour ground
Their accents did resound.
So forth those joyous birds did pass along,
Adown the Lea, that to them murmured low,
As he would speak, but that he lacked a tongue,
Yet did by signs his glad affection show,
Making his stream run slow.
And all the fowl which in his flood did dwell
Gan flock about those twain, that did excel
The rest, so far as Cynthia doth shend
The lesser stars. So they, enrangéd well,
Did on those two attend,
And their best service lend
Against their wedding day, which was not long:
Sweet Thames! run softly, till I end my song.

At length they all to merry London came,
To merry London, my most kindly nurse,
That to me gave this life's first native source,
Though from another place I take my name,
An house of ancient fame:
There, when they came whereas those bricky towers,
The which on Thames' broad aged back do ride,

Where now the studious lawyers have their bowers,
There whilome wont the Templar Knights to bide,
Till they decayed through pride:
Next whereunto there stands a stately place,
Where oft I gained gifts and goodly grace
Of that great lord which therein wont to dwell,
Whose want too well now feels my friendless case;
But ah! here fits not well
Old woes, but joys, to tell
Against the bridal day, which is not long:
Sweet Thames! run softly, till I end my song.

Yet therein now doth lodge a noble peer,
Great England's glory, and the world's wide wonder,
Whose dreadful name late through all Spain did thunder,
And Hercules' two pillars standing near
Did make to quake and fear:
Fair branch of honour, flower of chivalry!
That fillest England with thy triumph's fame,
Joy have thou of thy noble victory,
And endless happiness of thine own name
That promiseth the same;
That, through thy prowess and victorious arms,
Thy country may be freed from foreign harms;
And great Eliza's glorious name may ring
Through all the world, filled with thy wide alarms,
Which some brave muse may sing
To ages following,
Upon the bridal day, which is not long:
Sweet Thames! run softly, till I end my song.

From those high towers this noble lord issuing,
Like radiant Hesper, when his golden hair
In th' ocean billows he hath bathed fair,
Descended to the river's open viewing,

With a great train ensuing.
Above the rest were goodly to be seen
Two gentle knights of lovely face and feature,
Beseeming well the bower of any queen,
With gifts of wit, and ornaments of nature,
Fit for so goodly stature,
That like the twins of Jove they seemed in sight,
Which deck the baldrick of the heavens bright:
They two, forth pacing to the river's side,
Received those two fair brides, their love's delight;
Which, at th' appointed tide,
Each one did make his bride:
Against their bridal day, which is not long,
Sweet Thames! run softly, till I end my song.

Thames Doth the Medway Wed
From The Faerie Queene

WHEN HE WAS still in his twenties, long before he had written any of his major works, Edmund Spenser began work on a nuptial poem for the union of rivers. In 1580 he described his "Epithalamion Thamesis" in a letter to his friend Gabriel Harvey:

> For in setting forth the marriage of the Thames: I shewe his first beginning, and offspring, and all the countrey, that he passeth thorough, and also describe all the Rivers throughout Englande whyche came to this Wedding, and their righte names, and right passage, &c. A worke beleeve me, of much labour, wherein notwithstanding Master *Holinshed* hath muche furthered and advantaged me, who therein hath bestowed singular paines, in searching oute their firste heades, and sources: and also in tracing, and dogging out all their Course, til they fall into the Sea.

We don't know whether young Spenser finished the poem or not, but in the second part of his great romantic epic, *The Faerie Queene* (1596), there appears a canto (xi, in Book IV) which is probably a revision of the poem he described in the letter. The union of rivers here serves the function of dramatizing the theme of Book IV—Friendship, the operation in man's world of a harmonizing and unifying principle of cosmic love.

Mutability and the relation of order to chaos, of a moment in time to eternity, is a basic theme in all of Spenser's works. As Thomas P. Roche, Jr., has noted, although it is not stated explicitly in the canto, the reader knows that this marriage must dissolve itself in the multiplicity of the sea. He knows that this act of union will occur and dissolve again and again. Ultimately, he knows from his observation of the physical world that the act of union and dissolution are the same and inseparable.

> Marinell's former wound is healed,
>   he comes to Proteus hall,
> Where Thames doth the Medway wed,
>   and feasts the Sea-gods all.

It fortuned then, a solemn feast was there
    To all the Sea-gods and their fruitful seed,
    In honour of the spousals, which then were
    Betwixt the *Medway* and the *Thames* agreed.
    Long had the Thames (as we in records read)
    Before that day her wooed to his bed;
    But the proud Nymph would for no worldly meed,
    Nor no entreaty to his love be led;
Till now at last relenting, she to him was wed.

So both agreed, that this their bridal feast
    Should for the Gods in Proteus' house be made;
    To which they all repaired, both most and least,
    As well which in the mighty Ocean trade,
    As that in rivers swim, or brooks do wade.

All which not if an hundred tongues to tell,
And hundred mouths, and voice of brass I had
And endless memory, that mote excel,
In order as they came, could I recount them well.

Help therefore, O thou sacred imp of Jove,
The nurseling of Dame Memory his dear,
To whom those rolls, laid up in heaven above,
And records of antiquity appear,
To which no wit of man may comen near;
Help me to tell the names of all those floods,
And all those Nymphs, which then assembled were
To that great banquet of the watery Gods,
And all their sundry kinds, and all their hid abodes.

First came Neptune with his threeforked mace,
That rules the Seas, and makes them rise or fall;
His dewy locks did drop with brine apace,
Under his Diadem imperial:
And by his side his Queene with coronall,
Fair Amphitrite, most divinely fair,
Whose ivory shoulders weren covered all
As with a robe, with her own silver hair,
And decked with pearls, which th' Indian seas for her prepare.

These marchéd far afore the other crew;
And all the way before them as they went,
Triton his trumpet shrill before them blew,
For goodly triumph and great jolliment,
That made the rocks to roar, as they were rent.
And after them the royal issue came,
Which of them sprung by lineal descent:
First the Sea-gods, which to themselves do claim
The power to rule the billows, and the waves to tame.

EDMUND SPENSER

And after him the famous rivers came
   Which do the earth enrich and beautify:
   The fertile Nile, which creatures new doth frame;
   Long Rhodanus, whose source springs from the sky;
   Fair Ister, flowing from the mountains high
   Divine Scamander, purpled yet with blood
   Of Greeks and Trojans, which therein did die,
   Pactolus glist'ring with his golden flood,
And Tigris fierce, whose streams of none may be withstood.

. . . . . .

So went he playing on the watery plain.
   Soon after whom the lovely Bridegroom came,
   The noble Thamis, with all his goodly train,
   But him before there went, as best became,
   His ancient parents, namely th' ancient Thame.
   But much more agéd was his wife then he,
   The Ouze, whom men do Isis rightly name;
   Full weak and crooked creature seemed she,
And almost blind through eld, that scarce her way could see.

. . . . . .

Then came the Bride, the lovely Medua came,
   Clad in a vesture of unknown gear,
   And uncouth fashion, yet her well became;
   That seemed like silver, sprinkled here and there
   With glittering spangs, that did like stars appear,
   And waved upon, like water Chamelot
   To hide the metal, which yet every where
   Bewrayed it self, to let men plainly wot
It was no mortal work, that seemed and yet was not.

Her goodly locks adown her back did flow
    Unto her waist, with flowers bescatteréd,
    The which ambrosial odours forth did throw
    To all about, and all her shoulders spread
    As a new spring; and likewise on her head
    A chapelet of sundry flowers she wore
    From under which the dewy humour shed
    Did trickle down her hair, like to the hoar
Congealéd little drops, which do the morn adore.

On her, two pretty handmaids did attend,
    One called the Theise, the other called the Crane;
    Which on her waited, things amiss to mend,
    And both behind upheld her spreading train;
    Under the which, her feet appearéd plain,
    Her silver feet, fair washed against this day:
    And her before there pacéd Pages twain,
    Both clad in colours like, and like array,
The Doune and eke the Frith, both which prepared her way.

. . . . .

All these the daughters of old Nereus were,
    Which have the sea in charge to them assigned,
    To rule his tides, and surges to uprear,
    To bring forth storms, or fast them to upbind,
    And sailors save from wrecks of wrathful wind.
    And yet besides three thousand more there were
    Of th' Oceans seed, but Jove's and Phoebus' kind;
    The which in floods and fountains do appear,
And all mankind do nourish with their waters clear.

The which, more eath it were for mortal wight,
    To tell the sands, or count the stars on high

Or ought more hard, than think to reckon right.
But well I wote, that these which I descry,
Were present at this great solemnity:
And there amongst the rest, the mother was
Of luckless Marinell Cymodoce.
Which, for my Muse her self now tiréd has
Unto another Canto I will overpass.

* * *

MICHAEL DRAYTON, 1563-1631

Prothalamion

From *The Muses Elizium*

IN THE EIGHTH Nymphall of this work, Michael Drayton creates a delightful cast of fairy characters, friends of the bride, who chat engagingly of the wedding preparations. They refer to a number of bridal customs still common in the Renaissance, including breaking the wedding cake over the bride's head at the nuptial feast, and later—in the bridal chamber—the snatching of the bride's garters and the bridegroom's points (laces attaching the hose to the doublet), the scattering of nuts.

CLAIA

This day must Tita married be:
Come, Nymphs, this nuptial let us see.

MERTILLA

But is it certain, that you say?
Will she wed the noble fay?

CLORIS

Sprinkle the dainty flowers with dews,
Such as the Gods at banquets use:
Let herbs and weeds turn all to roses,
And make proud the posts with posies:
Shoot your sweets into the air:
Charge the morning to be fair.

CLAIA, MERTILLA

For our Tita is this day
To be married to a fay. . . .

CLORIS

Summon all the sweets that are,
To this nuptial to repair;
Till with their throng themselves they smother,
Strongly stifling one another;
And at last they all consume,
And vanish in one rich perfume. . . .

MERTILLA

But coming back when she is wed,
Who breaks the cake above her head?

CLAIA

That shall Mertilla, for she's tallest,
And our Tita is the smallest.

CLORIS

Violins, strike up aloud;
Ply the gittern, scour the crowd:

MICHAEL DRAYTON

Let the nimble hand belabour
The whistling pipe and drumling tabor:
To the full the bagpipe rack,
Till the swelling leather crack.

MERTILLA, CLAIA

For our Tita is this day
Married to a noble fay.

CLAIA

But when to dine she takes her seat,
What shall be our Tita's meat?

MERTILLA

The Gods this feast, as to begin
Have sent of their ambrosia in.

CLORIS

Then serve we up the straw's rich berry,
The respas, and Elizian cherry;
The virgin honey from the flowers
In Hybla, wrought in Flora's bowers;
Full bowls of nectar, and no girl
Carouse but in dissolved pearl.

MERTILLA, CLAIA

For our Tita is this day
Married to a noble fay.

CLAIA

But when night comes, and she must go
To bed, dear nymphs, what must we do?

Part III: Renaissance to 1900

MERTILLA

In the posset must be brought,
And points be from the bridegroom caught.

CLORIS

In masques, in dances, and delight,
And rare banquets spend the night:
Then about the room we ramble,
Scatter nuts and for them scamble:
Over stools and tables tumble,
Never think of noise nor rumble.

MERTILLA,
CLAIA

For our Tita is this day
Married to a noble fay.

* * *

WILLIAM SHAKESPEARE, 1564-1616

Come, Gentle Night

From *Romeo and Juliet* (Act III, Sc. ii)

Gallop apace, you fiery-footed steeds,
Towards Phoebus' lodging: such a waggoner
As Phaethon would whip you to the west,
And bring in cloudy night immediately.—
Spread thy close curtain, love-performing night,
That runaway's eyes may wink, and Romeo

(130)

Leap to these arms, untalk'd of and unseen.—
Lovers can see to do their amorous rites
By their own beauties; or, if love be blind,
It best agrees with night. Come, civil night,
Thou sober-suited matron, all in black,
And learn me how to lose a winning match,
Play'd for a pair of stainless maidenhoods.
Hood my unmann'd blood bating in my cheeks
With thy black mantle, till strange love grown bold
Think true love acted simple modesty.
Come, night, come, Romeo, come, thou day in night;
For thou wilt lie upon the wings of night
Whiter than new snow on a raven's back.
Come, gentle night, come, loving, black-brow'd night,
Give me my Romeo; and, when he shall die,
Take him and cut him out in little stars,
And he will make the face of heaven so fine
That all the world will be in love with night
And pay no worship to the garish sun.—
O, I have bought the mansion of a love,
But not possess'd it, and, though I am sold,
Not yet enjoy'd; so tedious is this day
As is the night before some festival
To an impatient child that hath new robes
And may not wear them.

High Wedlock Then Be Honoured
From *As You Like It* (Act V, Sc. iv)

Enter Hymen, Rosalind, and Celia. Still music

HYMEN

Then is there mirth in heaven
When earthly things made even
   Atone together.

Good Duke, receive thy daughter;
Hymen from heaven brought her,
  Yea, brought her hither,
That thou mightst join her hand with his
Whose heart within his bosom is.

ROSALIND [*to Duke Senior*]

To you I give myself, for I am yours.
       [*To Orlando*]
To you I give myself, for I am yours.

DUKE SENIOR

If there be truth in sight, you are my daughter.

ORLANDO

If there be truth in sight, you are my Rosalind.

PHEBE

If sight and shape be true,
Why then, my love adieu!

ROSALIND

I'll have no father, if you be not he. [*To Duke*]
I'll have no husband, if you be not he. [*To Orlando*]
Nor ne'er wed woman, if you be not she. [*To Phebe*]

HYMEN

Peace ho! I bar confusion.
'Tis I must make conclusion
  Of these most strange events.
Here's eight that must take hands
To join in Hymen's bands,
  If truth holds true contents.

WILLIAM SHAKESPEARE

[*To Orlando and Rosalind*]
You and you no cross shall part.
[*To Oliver and Celia*]
You and you are heart in heart.
[*To Phebe*]
You to his love must accord,
Or have a woman to your lord.
[*To Touchstone and Audrey*]
You and you are sure together
As the winter to foul weather.
Whiles a wedlock hymn we sing,
Feed yourselves with questioning,
That reason wonder may diminish
How thus we met, and these things finish.

Song

Wedding is great Juno's crown—
　O blessed bond of board and bed!
'Tis Hymen peoples every town;
　High wedlock then be honoured.
Honour, high honour, and renown
To Hymen, god of every town!

Blessings on the Bride-Bed

From *A Midsummer Night's Dream* (Act V, Sc. i)

Enter Oberon and Titania, with their Train

OBERON

Through the house give glimmering light
　By the dead and drowsy fire;

(133)

Every elf and fairy sprite
   Hop as light as bird from brier
And this ditty after me
Sing and dance it trippingly.

TITANIA

First, rehearse your song by rote,
To each word a warbling note:
Hand in hand, with fairy grace,
Will we sing, and bless this place.
Song and dance

OBERON

Now, until the break of day,
Through this house each fairy stray.
To the best bride-bed will we,
Which by us shall blessed be;
And the issue there create
Ever shall be fortunate.
So shall all the couples three
Ever true in loving be;
And the blots of Nature's hand
Shall not in their issue stand:
Never mole, hare-lip, nor scar,
Nor mark prodigious, such as are
Despised in nativity,
Shall upon their children be.
With this field-dew consecrate,
Every fairy take his gait,
And each several chamber bless,
Through this palace, with sweet peace;
Ever shall in safety rest,
And the owner of it blest.

WILLIAM SHAKESPEARE

Trip away;
Make no stay;
Meet me all by break of day.

Honour, Riches, Marriage Blessing
From *The Tempest* (Act IV, Sc. i)

CERES

Highest queen of state,
Great Juno, comes; I know her by her gait.
Enter Juno

JUNO

How does my bounteous sister? Go with me
To bless this twain, that they may prosperous be
And honoured in their issue.
Song

JUNO

Honour, riches, marriage blessing,
Long continuance, and increasing,
Hourly joys be still upon you!
Juno sings her blessings on you.

CERES

Earth's increase, foison plenty,
Barns and garners never empty,
Vines with clust'ring bunches growing,
Plants with goodly burden bowing;
Spring come to you at the farthest
In the very end of harvest!
Scarcity and want shall shun you,
Ceres' blessing so is on you.

FERDINAND

This is a most majestic vision, and
Harmonious charmingly. May I be bold
To think these spirits?

PROSPERO

   Spirits, which by mine art
I have from their confines called to enact
My present fancies.

FERDINAND

   Let me live here ever!
So rare a wond'red father and a wise
Makes this place Paradise.
Juno and Ceres whisper, and send Iris on employment

PROSPERO

   Sweet now, silence!
Juno and Ceres whisper seriously.
There's something else to do. Hush and be mute,
Or else our spell is marred.

IRIS

You nymphs, called Naiads, of the wind'ring brooks,
With your sedged crowns and ever-harmless looks,
Leave your crisp channels, and on this green land
Answer your summons. Juno does command.
Come, temperate nymphs, and help to celebrate
A contract of true love. Be not too late.

Enter certain Nymphs

You sunburned sicklemen, of August weary,
Come hither from the furrow and be merry.

Make holiday. Your rye-straw hats put on,
And these fresh nymphs encounter every one
In country footing.

[*Enter certain Reapers, properly habited. They join with the Nymphs in a graceful dance; towards the end whereof Prospero starts suddenly and speaks; after which, to a strange, hollow, and confused noise, they heavily vanish.*]

* * *

WILLIAM SHAKESPEARE *or* JOHN FLETCHER, 1579-1625

Roses, Their Sharp Spines Being Gone

From *The Two Noble Kinsmen* (Act I, Sc. i)

Roses, their sharp spines being gone,
Not royal in their smells alone,
But in their hue;
Maiden-pinks, of odour faint,
Daisies smell-less, yet most quaint,
And sweet thyme true;

Primrose, firstborn child of Ver,
Merry Spring-time's harbinger,
With her bells dim;
Oxlips in their cradles growing,
Marigolds on death-beds blowing,
Lark-heels trim;

All dear Nature's children sweet
Lie fore bride and bridegroom's feet,
Blessing their sense!
Not an angel of the air,
Bird melodious, or bird fair,
Be absent hence.

The crow, the slanderous cuckoo, nor
The boding raven, nor chough hoar,
Nor chattering pie,
May on our bridehouse perch or sing,
Or with them any discord bring,
But from it fly!

* * *

JOHN DONNE, 1572-1631

Epithalamion Made at Lincoln's Inn

The sunbeams in the east are spread,
Leave, leave, fair bride, your solitary bed,
  No more shall you return to it alone,
It nurseth sadness, and your body's print,
Like to a grave, the yielding down doth dint;
  You and your other you meet there anon;
  Put forth, put forth that warm balm-breathing thigh,
Which when next time you in these sheets will smother,
  There it must meet another,
  Which never was, but must be, oft, more nigh;
Come glad from thence, go gladder than you came,
Today put on perfection, and a woman's name.

JOHN DONNE

Daughters of London, you which be
Our golden mines, and furnish'd treasury,
   You which are Angels, yet still bring with you
Thousands of angels on your marriage days,
Help with your presence and devise to praise
   These rites, which also unto you grow due;
   Conceitedly dress her, and be assign'd,
By you, fit place for every flower and jewel,
   Make her for love fit fuel
      As gay as Flora, and as rich as Ind;
So may she fair, rich, glad, and in nothing lame,
Today put on perfection, and a woman's name.

And you frolic patricians,
Sons of these senators, wealth's deep oceans,
   Ye painted courtiers, barrels of others' wits,
Ye country men, who but your beasts love none,
Ye of those fellowships whereof he's one,
   Of study and play made strange hermaphrodites,
   Here shine; this bridegroom to the temple bring.
Lo, in yon path which store of straw'd flowers graceth,
   The sober virgin paceth;
      Except my sight fail, 'tis no other thing;
Weep not nor blush, here is no grief nor shame,
Today put on perfection, and a woman's name.

Thy two-leav'd gates, fair temple unfold,
And these two in thy sacred bosom hold,
   Till, mystically join'd, but one they be;
Then may thy lean and hunger-starvèd womb
Long time expect their bodies and their tomb,
   Long after their own parents fatten thee.
   All elder claims, and all cold barrenness,
All yielding to new loves be far forever,
   Which might these two dissever,
      All ways all the other may each one possess;

For, the best Bride, best worthy of praise and fame,
Today puts on perfection, and a woman's name.

Oh winter days bring much delight,
Not for themselves, but for they soon bring night;
　Other sweets wait thee than these diverse meats,
Other disports than dancing jollities,
Other love tricks than glancing with the eyes,
　But that the sun still in our half sphere sweats;
　　He flies in winter, but he now stands still.
Yet shadows turn; noon point he hath attain'd,
　His steeds will be restrain'd,
　　But gallop lively down the western hill;
Thou shalt, when he hath run the world's half frame,
Tonight put on perfection, and a woman's name.

The amorous evening star is rose,
Why then should not our amorous star enclose
　Herself in her wish'd bed? Release your strings,
Musicians, and dancers take some truce
With these your pleasing labours, for great use
　As much weariness as perfection brings;
　　You, and not only you, but all toil'd beasts
Rest duly; at night all their toils are dispensed;
But in their beds commenced
　　Are other labors, and more dainty feasts;
She goes a maid, who, lest she turn the same,
Tonight puts on perfection, and a woman's name.

Thy virgin's girdle now untie,
And in thy nuptial bed (love's altar) lie
　A pleasing sacrifice; now dispossess
Thee of these chains and robes which were put on
To adorn the day, not thee; for thou, alone,
　Like virtue and truth, art best in nakedness;

> This bed is only to virginity
A grave, but to a better state, a cradle;
Till now thou wast but able
> To be what now thou art; then that by thee
No more be said, *I may be,* but, *I am,*
Tonight put on perfection, and a woman's name.

Even like a faithful man content
That this life for a better should be spent,
> So she a mother's rich style doth prefer,
And at the bridegroom's wish'd approach doth lie
Like an appointed lamb, when tenderly
> The priest comes on his knees to embowel her;
> Now sleep or watch with more joy; and O light
Of heaven, tomorrow rise thou hot and early;
This Sun will love so dearly
> Her rest, that long, long we shall want her sight;
Wonders are wrought, for she which had no maim,
Tonight puts on perfection, and a woman's name.

An Epithalamion, or Marriage Song

On the Lady Elizabeth, and Count Palatine Being Married on St. Valentine's Day

I

Hail Bishop Valentine, whose day this is,
> All the air is thy diocese,
> And all the chirping choristers
And other birds are thy parishioners;
> Thou marriest every year
The lyric lark, and the grave whispering dove,
The sparrow that neglects his life for love,
The household bird with the red stomacher,
> Thou mak'st the black bird speed as soon

As doth the goldfinch, or the halcyon;
The husband cock looks out, and straight is sped,
And meets his wife, which brings her feather-bed.
This day more cheerfully than ever shine,
This day, which might enflame thyself, old Valentine.

II

Till now, thou warm'dst with multiplying loves,
    Two larks, two sparrows, or two doves;
      All that is nothing unto this,
For thou this day couplest two Phoenixes;
      Thou mak'st a taper see
What the sun never saw, and what the Ark
(Which was of fowls, and beasts, the cage, and park)
Did not contain, one bed contains, through thee,
    Two Phoenixes, whose joinéd breasts
Are unto one another mutual nests,
Where motion kindles such fires as shall give
Young Phoenixes, and yet the old shall live.
Whose love and courage never shall decline,
But make the whole year through, thy day, O Valentine.

III

Up then fair Phoenix Bride, frustrate the Sun,
    Thyself from thine affection
    Takest warmth enough, and from thine eye
All lesser birds will take their jollity.
    Up, up, fair Bride, and call
Thy stars from out their several boxes, take
Thy rubies, pearls, and diamonds forth, and make
Thyself a constellation of them all,
    And by their blazing, signify
That a great Princess falls, but doth not die;

Be thou a new star, that to us portends
Ends of much wonder; and be thou those ends.
Since thou dost this day in new glory shine,
May all men date records from this thy Valentine.

IV

Come forth, come forth, and as one glorious flame
    Meeting another, grows the same,
    So meet thy Frederick, and so
To an unseparable union grow.
    Since separation
Falls not on such things as are infinite,
Nor things which are but one, can disunite,
You are twice inseparable, great, and one;
    Go then to where the Bishop stays
To make you one, his way, which divers ways
Must be effected; and when all is past,
And that you are one, by hearts and hands made fast,
You two have one way left, yourselves to entwine,
Besides this Bishop's knot, or Bishop Valentine.

V

But oh, what ails the Sun, that here he stays
    Longer today, than other days?
    Stays he new light from these to get?
And finding here such store, is loath to set?
    And why do you two walk,
So slowly pac'd in this procession?
Is all your care but to be look'd upon,
And be to others spectacle, and talk?
    The feast, with gluttonous delays,
Is eaten, and too long their meat they praise,
The masquers come too late, and I think will stay,
Like fairies, till the cock crow them away.

Alas, did not antiquity assign
A night, as well as day, to thee, O Valentine?

VI

They did, and night is come; and yet we see
    Formalities retarding thee.
    What mean these ladies, which (as though
They were to take a clock in pieces) go
    So nicely about the bride;
A bride, before a good night could be said,
Should vanish from her clothes into her bed,
As souls from bodies steal and are not spied.
    But now she is laid, what though she be?
Yet there are more delays, for where is he?
He comes, and passes through sphere after sphere,
First her sheets, then her arms, then anywhere.
Let not this day, then, but this night be thine,
Thy day was but the eve to this, O Valentine.

VII

Here lies a she-Sun, and a he-Moon here,
    She gives the best light to his sphere,
    Or each is both, and all, and so
They unto one another nothing owe,
    And yet they do, but are
So just and rich in that coin which they pay,
That neither would, nor needs forbear, nor stay;
Neither desires to be spar'd, nor to spare,
    They quickly pay their debt, and then
Take no acquittances, but pay again;
They pay, they give, they lend, and so let fall
No such occasion to be liberal.
More truth, more courage in these two do shine,
Then all thy turtles have, and sparrows, Valentine.

VIII

And by this act of these two Phoenixes
    Nature again restored is,
    For since these two are two no more,
There's but one Phoenix still, as was before.
    Rest now at last, and we
As satyrs watch the Sun's uprise, will stay
Waiting, when your eyes open'd, let out day,
Only desir'd, because your face we see;
    Others near you shall whispering speak,
And wagers lay, at which side day will break,
And win by observing, then, whose hand it is
That opens first a curtain, hers or his;
This will be tried tomorrow after nine,
Till which hour, we thy day enlarge, O Valentine.

* * *

BEN JONSON, 1573-1637

Glad Time Is at His Point Arrived
From *Masque of Hymen*

Glad time is at his point arrived,
For which love's hopes were so long lived.
    Lead! Hymen, lead away!
    And let no object stay,
    Nor banquets, but sweet kisses,
    The turtles from their blisses:
    'Tis Cupid calls to arm;
    And this his last alarm.

Shrink not, soft virgin, you will love
Anon, what you so fear to prove.
    This is no killing war,
    To which you pressed are;
    But fair and gentle strife,
    Which lovers call their life.
    'Tis Cupid calls to arm;
    And this his last alarm.

Help, youths and virgins, help to sing
The prize, which Hymen here doth bring;
    And did so lately rap
    From forth the mother's lap,
    To place her by that side,
    Where she must long abide.
    On Hymen, Hymen call!
    This night is Hymen's all.

See! Hesperus is yet in view.
What star can so deserve of you?
    Whose light doth still adorn
    Your bride, that ere the morn
    Shall far more perfect be,
    And rise as bright as he;
    When, like to him, her name
    Is changed, but not her flame.

Haste, tender lady, and adventer;
The covetous house would have you enter,
    That it might wealthy be,
    And you, her mistress, see:
    Haste your own good to meet;
    And lift your golden feet
    Above the threshold high,
    With prosperous augury.

Now, youths, let go your pretty arms;
The place within chants other charms.
    Whole showers of roses flow;
    And violets seem to grow,
    Strewed in the chamber there,
    As Venus' mead it were.
    On Hymen, Hymen call!
    This night is Hymen's all.

Good matrons, that so well are known
To aged husbands of your own,
    Place you our bride to-night;
    And snatch away the light:
    That she not hide it dead
    Beneath her spouse's bed;
    Nor he reserve the same
    To help the funeral flame.

So! now you may admit him in;
The act he covets is no sin,
    But chaste and holy love,
    Which Hymen doth approve:
    Without whose hallowing fires,
    All aims are base desires.
    On Hymen, Hymen call!
    This night is Hymen's all.

Now, free from vulgar spite or noise,
May you enjoy your mutual joys;
    Now you no fear controls,
    But lips may mingle souls;
    And soft embraces bind
    To each the other's mind;
    Which may no power untie,
    Till one or both must die!

And look, before you yield to slumber,
That your delights be drawn past number;
      Joys, got with strife, increase.
      Affect no sleepy peace;
      But keep the bride's fair eyes
      Awake with her own cries,
      Which are but maiden fears:
      And kisses dry such tears.

Then coin 'em twixt your lips so sweet,
And let not cockles closer meet;
      Nor may your murmuring loves
      Be drowned by Cypris' doves:
      Let ivy not so bind,
      As when your arms are twined:
      That you may both ere day
      Rise perfect every way.

And Juno, whose great powers protect
The marriage bed, with good effect
      The labour of this night
      Bless thou, for future light:
      And thou, thy happy charge,
      Glad Genius, enlarge;
      That they may both ere day
      Rise perfect every way.

And Venus, thou, with timely seed,
Which may their after-comforts breed,
      Inform the gentle womb;
      Nor let it prove a tomb:
      But ere ten months be wasted,
      The birth by Cynthia hasted.
      So may they both ere day
      Rise perfect every way.

And when the babe to light is shown,
Let it be like each parent known;
    Much of the father's face,
    More of the mother's grace;
    And either grandsire's spirit,
    And fame let it inherit:
    That men may bless th' embraces
    That joined two such races.

Cease, youths and virgins, you have done;
Shut fast the door; and as they soon
    To their perfection haste,
    So may their ardours last.
    So either's strength outlive
    All loss that age can give;
    And though full years be told,
    Their forms grow slowly old.

Up, Youths and Virgins, Up, and Praise
From *Masque of Cupid*

Up, youths and virgins, up, and praise
The God whose nights outshine his days;
   Hymen, whose hallowed rites
Could never boast of brighter lights;
   Whose bands pass liberty.
Two of your troop, that with the morn were free,
   Are now waged to his war.
     And what they are,
  If you'll perfection see,
    Yourselves must be.
Shine, Hesperus, shine forth, thou wished star!

What joy or honours can compare
With holy nuptials, when they are
   Made out of equal parts
Of years, of states, of hands, of hearts!
   When in the happy choice
The spouse and spoused have the foremost voice!
    Such, glad of Hymen's war,
      Live what they are,
    And long perfection see:
      And such ours be.
Shine, Hesperus, shine forth, thou wished star!

The solemn state of this one night
Were fit to last an age's light;
   But there are rites behind
Have less of state, but more of kind:
   Love's wealthy crop of kisses,
And fruitful harvest of his mother's blisses.
    Sound then to Hymen's war:
      That what these are,
    Who will perfection see,
      May haste to be.
Shine, Hesperus, shine forth, thou wished star!

Love's commonwealth consists of toys;
His council are those antic boys,
   Games, Laughter, Sports, Delights,
That triumph with him on these nights;
   To whom we must give way,
For now their reign begins, and lasts till day.
    They sweeten Hymen's war,
      And in that jar,
    Make all that married be
      Perfection see.
Shine, Hesperus, shine forth, thou wished star!

Why stays the bridegroom to invade
Her that would be a matron made?
   Good-night whilst yet we may
Good-night to you a virgin say:
   To-morrow rise the same
Your mother is, and use a nobler name.
   Speed well in Hymen's war,
     That what you are,
   By your perfection we
     And all may see.
Shine, Hesperus, shine forth, thou wished star!

To-night is Venus' vigil kept.
This night no bridegroom ever slept;
   And if the fair bride do,
The married say, 'tis his fault too.
   Wake then, and let your lights
Wake too; for they'll tell nothing of your nights,
   But that in Hymen's war
     You perfect are.
   And such perfection we
     Do pray should be.
Shine, Hesperus, shine forth, thou wished star!

That ere the rosy-fingered morn
Behold nine moons, there may be born
   A babe t' uphold the fame
Of Ratcliffe's blood and Ramsey's name:
   That may, in his great seed,
Wear the long honours of his father's deed.
   Such fruits of Hymen's war
     Most perfect are;
   And all perfection we
     Wish you should see.
Shine, Hesperus, shine forth, thou wished star!

Part III: Renaissance to 1900

JOHN WEBSTER, c. 1580-1625

Hark, Now Everything Is Still
From *The Duchess of Malfi* (Act IV, Sc. ii)

IN THIS "anti"-nuptial poem the duchess is instructed to prepare for her death at the hands of her cruel brothers. Her preparations are like those of a bride for her wedding, including the ceremonial bathing of her feet. The madman's song precedes the nuptial instructions.

[*Here this Song is sung by a Madman to a dismal kind of music*]

>Oh, let us howl some heavy note,
> Some deadly dogged howl,
>Sounding as from the threatening throat
> Of beasts and fatal fowl!
>As ravens, screech-owls, bulls, and bears,
> We'll bell, and bawl our parts,
>Till irksome noise have cloy'd your ears
> And corrosived your hearts.
>At last, whenas our quire wants breath,
> Our bodies being blest,
>We'll sing, like swans, to welcome death,
> And die in love and rest.

. . . . .

>Hark, now every thing is still
>The screech-owl and the whistler shrill
>Call upon our dame aloud,
>And bid her quickly don her shroud!
>Much you had of land and rent:

Your length in clay's now competent:
A long war disturb'd your mind;
Here your perfect peace is sign'd.
Of what is 't fools make such vain keeping?
Sin their conception, their birth weeping,
Their life a general mist of error,
Their death a hideous storm of terror.
Strew your hair with powders sweet,
Don clean linen, bathe your feet,
And (the foul fiend more to check)
A crucifix let bless your neck:
'Tis now full tide 'tween night and day;
End your groan, and come away.

* * *

ROBERT HERRICK, 1591-1674

An Epithalamie to Sir Thomas Southwell and His Lady

Now, now's the time so oft by truth
Promised should come to crown your youth.
    Then, fair ones, do not wrong
    Your joys by staying long:
    Or let Love's fire go out,
    By ling'ring thus in doubt:
    But learn that time once lost
    Is ne'er redeemed by cost.
Then away! come Hymen, guide
To the bed the bashful bride!

Is it (sweet maid) your fault, these holy
Bridal rites go on so slowly?
    Dear, is it this you dread,
    The loss of maidenhead?
    Believe me; you will most
    Esteem it when 'tis lost:
    Then it no longer keep,
    Lest issue lie asleep.
Then away! come Hymen, guide
To the bed the bashful bride!

These precious-pearly-purling tears
But spring from ceremonious fears,
    And 'tis but native shame
    That hides the loving flame:
    And may a while controul
    The soft and amorous soul;
    But yet, Love's fire will waste
    Such bashfulness at last.
Then away! come Hymen, guide
To the bed the bashful bride!

Night now hath watched herself half blind;
Yet not a maidenhead resigned!
    'Tis strange ye will not fly
    To Love's sweet mystery.
    Might yon full moon the sweets
    Have, promised to your sheets;
    She soon would leave her sphere,
    To be admitted there.
Then away! come Hymen, guide
To the bed the bashful bride!

On, on devoutly, make no stay;
While Domiduca leads the way:

And Genius who attends
The bed for lucky ends:
With Juno goes the Hours,
And Graces strewing flowers:
And the boys with sweet tunes sing,
Hymen, O Hymen bring
Home the turtles; Hymen guide
To the bed the bashful bride!

Behold! how Hymen's taper-light
Shews you how much is spent of night.
    See, see the bridegroom's torch
    Half wasted in the porch.
    And now those tapers five,
    That shew the womb shall thrive:
    Their silvery flames advance,
    To tell all prosperous chance
Still shall crown the happy life
Of the goodman and the wife.

Move forward then your rosy feet,
And make whate'er they touch turn sweet.
    May all, like flowery meads
    Smell, where your soft foot treads;
    And every thing assume
    To it, the like perfume
    As Zephirus, when he 'spires
    Through woodbine and sweet-briars.
Then away! come Hymen, guide
To the bed the bashful bride!

And now the yellow veil, at last,
Over her fragrant cheek is cast.
    Now seems she to express
    A bashful willingness,

Shewing a heart consenting,
As with a will repenting.
  Then gently lead her on
  With wise suspicion;
For that matrons say, a measure
Of that passion sweetens pleasure.

You, you that be of her nearest kin,
Now o'er the threshold force her in.
  But to avert the worst,
  Let her, her fillets first
  Knit to the posts: this point
  Rememb'ring, to anoint
  The sides: for 'tis a charm
  Strong against future harm:
And the evil deads, the which
There was hidden by the witch.

O Venus! thou to whom is known
The best way how to loose the zone
  Of virgins; tell the maid
  She need not be afraid:
  And bid the youth apply
  Close kisses, if she cry:
  And charge, he not forbears
  Her, though she woo with tears.
Tell them, now they must adventer,
Since that Love and Night bid enter.

No fatal owl the bedstead keeps,
With direful notes to fright your sleeps:
  No Furies, here about,
  To put the tapers out,
  Watch, or did make the bed:
  'Tis omen full of dread:

> But all fair signs appear
> Within the chamber here.
> Juno here, far off, doth stand
> Cooling sleep with charming wand.
>
> Virgins, weep not; 'twill come, when,
> As she, so you'll be ripe for men.
> > Then grieve her not with saying,
> > She must no more a-maying:
> > Or by rose-buds divine,
> > Who'll be her Valentine.
> > Nor name those wanton reaks
> > Y'ave had at barley-breaks.
> But now kiss her, and thus say,
> Take time lady while ye may.
>
> Now bar the doors; the bridegroom puts
> The eager boys to gather nuts.
> > And now, both Love and Time
> > To their full height do climb:
> > O give them active heat
> > And moisture, both complete:
> > Fit organs for increase,
> > To keep and to release
> That, which may the honoured stem
> Circle with a diadem!
>
> And now, behold! the bed or couch
> That ne'er knew bride's or bridegroom's touch,
> > Feels in itself a fire;
> > And tickled with desire,
> > Pants with a downy breast,
> > As with a heart possest:
> > Shrugging as it did move,
> > Ev'n with the soul of love.

And, oh! had it but a tongue,
Doves, 'twould say, ye bill too long.

O enter, then! but see ye shun
A sleep, until the act be done.
    Let kisses, in their close,
    Breathe as the damask rose:
    Or sweet, as is that gum
    Doth from Panchaia come.
    Teach Nature now to know,
    Lips can make cherries grow
Sooner, than she, ever yet
In her wisdom could beget.

On your minutes, hours, days, months, years,
Drop the fat blessing of the spheres.
    That good, which Heaven can give
    To make you bravely live,
    Fall like a spangling dew,
    By day and night on you.
    May Fortune's lily hand
    Open at your command;
With all lucky birds to side
With the bridegroom, and the bride.

Let bounteous Fate your spindles full
Fill, and wind up, with whitest wool.
    Let them not cut the thread
    Of life, until ye bid.
    May death yet come at last;
    And not with desperate haste:
    But when ye both can say,
    Come, let us now away.
Be ye to the barn then borne,
Two, like two ripe shocks of corn.

ROBERT HERRICK

A Nuptial Song, or Epithalamie,
on Sir Clipseby Crew and His Lady

What's that we see from far? the spring of day
Bloomed from the East, or fair injewelled May
    Blown out of April; or some new
    Star filled with glory to our view,
        Reaching at Heaven,
To add a nobler planet to the seven?
    Say, or do we not descry
Some Goddess, in a cloud of tiffany
        To move, or rather the
    Emergent Venus from the sea?

'Tis she! 'tis she! or else some more divine
Enlightened substance; mark how from the shrine
    Of holy saint she paces on,
    Treading upon vermilion
        And amber; spice-
ing the chafed air with fumes of Paradise.
    Then come on, come on, and yield
A savour like unto a blessed field,
        When the bedabled morn
    Washes the golden ears of corn.

See where she comes; and smell how all the street
Breathes vineyards and pomegranates: O how sweet,
    As a fired altar, is each stone
    Perspiring powdered cinnamon.
        The Phoenix nest,
Built up of odours, burneth in her breast.
    Who therein would not consume
His soul to ash-heaps in that rich perfume?
        Bestroking Fate the while
    He burns to embers on the pile.

Hymen, O Hymen! tread the sacred ground;
Shew thy white feet, and head with marjoram crowned:
    Mount up thy flames, and let thy torch
    Display the bridegroom in the porch,
        In his desires
More towering, more disparkling than thy fires:
    Shew her how his eyes do turn
And roll about, and in their motions burn
        Their balls to cinders: haste,
    Or else to ashes he will waste!

Glide by the banks of virgins then, and pass
The showers of roses, lucky four-leaved grass:
    The while the crowd of younglings sing,
    And drown ye with a flowery Spring:
        While some repeat
Your praise, and bless you, sprinkling you with wheat:
    While that others do divine:
Blest is the bride on whom the sun doth shine;
        And thousands gladly wish
    You multiply as doth a fish.

And beauteous bride we do confess y' are wise,
In dealing forth these bashful jealousies:
    In Love's name do so; and a price
    Set on your self, by being nice:
        But yet take heed;
What now you seem, be not the same indeed,
    And turn apostate: Love will
Part of the way be met, or sit stone-still.
        On then, and though you slow-
    ly go, yet, howsoever, go.

And now y' are entered; see the codled cook
Runs from his torrid zone to pry, and look,

ROBERT HERRICK

    And bless his dainty mistress: see
    The aged point out, This is she,
        Who now must sway
The house (Love shield her!) with her yea and nay:
    And the smirk butler thinks it
Sin, in 's nap'ry not to express his wit;
        Each striving to devise
    Some gin, wherewith to catch your eyes.

To bed, to bed, kind turtles, now, and write
This the short'st day, and this the longest night!
    But yet too short for you: 'tis we
        Who count this night as long as three,
            Lying alone,
Telling the clock strike ten, eleven, twelve, one.
    Quickly, quickly, then prepare,
And let the young men and the bride-maids share
        Your garters; and their joints
    Encircle with the bridegroom's points.

By the bride's eyes, and by the teeming life
Of her green hopes, we charge ye, that no strife
    (Farther than gentleness tends) gets place
        Among ye, striving for her lace:
            O do not fall
Foul in these noble pastimes, lest ye call
    Discord in, and so divide
The youthful bridegroom and the fragrant bride:
        Which Love fore-fend; but spoken
    Be 't to your praise, no peace was broken.

Strip her of Spring-time, tender-whimpering-maids;
Now Autumn's come, when all those flowery aids
    Of her delays must end: dispose

That lady-smock, that pansy, and that rose
    Neatly apart;
But for prick-madam, and for gentle-heart,
    And soft maiden's-blush, the bride
Makes holy these; all others lay aside:
      Then strip her, or unto her
      Let him come, who dares undo her.

And to enchant ye more, see every where
About the roof a siren in a sphere,
    (As we think) singing to the din
    Of many a warbling cherubin:
      O mark ye how
The soul of Nature melts in numbers: now
    See, a thousand Cupids fly
To light their tapers at the bride's bright eye!
      To bed; or her they'll tire,
    Were she an element of fire.

And to your more bewitching, see, the proud
Plump bed bear up, and swelling like a cloud,
    Tempting the two too modest; can
    You see it brusle like a swan,
      And you be cold
To meet it, when it woos and seems to fold
    The arms to hug it? throw, throw
Yourselves into the mighty over-flow
      Of that white pride, and drown
    The night, with you, in floods of down!

The bed is ready, and the maze of Love
Looks for the treaders; every where is wove
    Wit and new mystery; read, and
    Put in practise, to understand
      And know each wile,

Each hieroglyphic of a kiss or smile;
    And do it to the full; reach
High in your own conceit, and some way teach
        Nature and Art, one more
      Play than they ever knew before.

If needs we must, for ceremony's sake,
Bless a sack-posset; luck go with it; take
    The night-charm quickly; you have spells,
    And magics for to end, and hells
        To pass; but such
And of such torture as no one would grutch
      To live therein for ever: frie
And consume, and grow again to die,
        And live, and in that case,
     Love the confusion of the place.

But since it must be done, despatch, and sew
Up in a sheet your bride; and what if so
      It be with rock or walls of brass
      Ye tower her up, as Danae was;
        Think you that this,
Or Hell itself a powerful bulwark is?
    I tell ye no; but like a
Bold bolt of thunder he will make his way,
      And rend the cloud, and throw
    The sheet about, like flakes of snow.

All now is husht in silence; Midwife-Moon,
With all her owl-eyed issue begs a boon
    Which you must grant; that's entrance; with
    Which extract all we can call pith
        And quintessence
Of planetary bodies; so commence,
    All fair constellations

    Looking upon ye, that two nations,
        Springing from two such fires,
    May blaze the virtue of their sires.

Connubii Flores,
or the Well-Wishes at Weddings

THIS HERRICK poem is a novelty in the tradition in that it consists of a series of songs sung not by two choruses as in Catullus's Carmen 62 but by a series of choruses—priests, young men, old men, virgins, shepherds, matrons, and finally all singing together. The priests ask that blessings may come to the couple as they go from the temple to their home, the young men ask that night may come soon, the virgins wish that the goddess of childbirth may give tender care to the bride as "her April hour draws near," the matrons and shepherds give practical advice on household chores, and the old men advise moderation in love, offering a series of well-worn proverbs.

CHORUS SACERDOTUM

    From the temple to your home
      May a thousand blessings come!
    And a sweet concurring stream
    Of all joys, to join with them.

CHORUS JUVENUM

      Happy day,
    Make no longer stay
        Here
      In thy sphere;
  But give thy place to night,
      That she,
      As thee,
      May be
Partaker of this sight.

ROBERT HERRICK

And since it was thy care
To see the younglings wed;
'Tis fit that Night, the pair,
Should see safe brought to bed.

CHORUS SENUM

Go to your banquet then, but use delight,
So as to rise still with an appetite.
Love is a thing most nice; and must be fed
To such a height, but never surfeited.
What is beyond the mean is ever ill:
'Tis best to feed Love, but not over-fill:
Go then discreetly to the bed of pleasure;
And this remember: Virtue keeps the measure.

CHORUS VIRGINUM

Lucky signs we have descried
To encourage on the bride;
And to these we have espied,
Not a kissing Cupid flies
Here about, but has his eyes,
To imply your love is wise.

CHORUS PASTORUM

Here we present a fleece
To make a piece
Of cloth;
Nor, fair, must you be loth
Your finger to apply
To housewifery.
Then, then begin
To spin:
And (sweetling) mark you, what a web will come
Into your chests, drawn by your painful thumb.

(165)

CHORUS MATRONARUM

Set you to your wheel, and wax
Rich by the ductile wool and flax.
Yarn is an income; and the housewife's thread
The larder fills with meat, the bin with bread.

CHORUS SENUM

Let wealth come in by comely thrift,
And not by any sordid shift:
    'Tis haste
    Makes waste;
Extremes have still their fault;
The softest fire makes the sweetest malt.
Who grips too hard the dry and slippery sand,
Holds none at all, or little, in his hand.

CHORUS VIRGINUM

Goddess of pleasure, youth, and peace,
Give them the blessing of increase:
And thou Lucina, that dost hear
The vows of those that children bear:
Whenas her April hour draws near,
Be thou then propitious there!

CHORUS JUVENUM

Far hence be all speech that may anger move:
Sweet words must nourish soft and gentle love.

CHORUS OMNIUM

Live in the love of doves, and, having told
The raven's years, go hence more ripe than old.

ROBERT HERRICK

A Nuptial Verse to Mistress Elizabeth Lee Now Lady Tracy

Spring with the lark, most comely bride, and meet
Your eager bridegroom with auspicious feet.
The morn's far spent; and the immortal sun
Corals his cheeks to see those rites not done.
Fie, lovely maid! Indeed you are too slow,
When to the temple Love should run, not go.
Dispatch your dressing then, and quickly wed:
Then feast and coy't a little; then to bed.
This day is Love's day; and this busy night
Is yours, in which you challenged are to fight
With such an armed, but such an easy foe,
As will if you yield, lie down conquered too.
The field is pitched; but such must be your wars,
As that your kisses must outvie the stars.
Fall down together vanquished both, and lie
Drowned in the blood of rubies there, not die.

The Entertainment: or, Porch-verse at the Marriage of Master Henry Northly, and the Most Witty Mistress Lettice Yard

Welcome! but yet no entrance, till we bless
   First you, then you, and both for white success.
Profane no Porch, young man and maid, for fear
Ye wrong the Threshold-God that keeps peace here:
Please him, and then all good luck will betide
You, the brisk bridegroom, you, the dainty bride.

Do all things sweetly, and in comely wise;
Put on your garlands first, then sacrifice:
That done; when both of you have seemly fed,
We'll call on Night to bring ye both to bed:
Where, being laid, all fair signs looking on,
Fish-like increase then to a million:
And millions of spring-times may ye have,
Which spent, one death bring to ye both one grave.

The Good-Night or Blessing

Blessings in abundance come
To the bride and to her groom;
May the bed and this short night
Know the fulness of delight!
Pleasures many here attend ye,
And, ere long, a boy Love send ye
Curled and comely, and so trim,
Maids in time may ravish him.
Thus a dew of graces fall
On ye both: good-night to all!

* * *

JOHN MILTON, 1608-1674

Hail, Wedded Love

From *Paradise Lost* (Book IV)

So passed they naked on, nor shunned the sight
Of God or Angel, for they thought no ill:
So hand in hand they passed, the loveliest pair
That ever since in love's embraces met—

JOHN MILTON

Adam the goodliest man of men since born
His sons; the fairest of her daughters Eve.
Under a tuft of shade that on a green
Stood whispering soft, by a fresh fountain-side,
They sat them down; and, after no more toil
Of their sweet gardening labour than sufficed
To recommend cool Zephyr, and make ease
More easy, wholesome thirst and appetite
More grateful, to their supper-fruits they fell—
Nectarine fruits, which the compliant boughs
Yielded them, sidelong as they sat recline
On the soft downy bank demasked with flowers.
The savoury pulp they chew, and in the rind,
Still as they thirsted, scoop the brimming stream;
Nor gentle purpose, nor endearing smiles
Wanted, nor youthful dalliance, as beseems
Fair couple linked in happy nuptial league,
Alone as they.

• • •

   Thus talking, hand in hand alone they passed
On to their blissful bower. It was a place
Chosen by the sovran Planter, when he framed
All things to Man's delightful use. The roof
Of thickest covert was inwoven shade,
Laurel and myrtle, and what higher grew
Of firm and fragrant leaf; on either side
Acanthus, and each odorous bushy shrub,
Fenced up the verdant wall; each beauteous flower,
Iris all hues, roses, and jessamine,
Reared high their flourished heads between, and
    wrought
Mosaic; under foot the violet,
Crocus, and hyacinth, with rich inlay
Broidered the ground, more coloured than with stone

Of costliest emblem. . . . Here, in close recess,
With flowers, garlands, and sweet-smelling herbs,
Espoused Eve decked first her nuptial bed,
And heavenly choirs the hymenaean sung,
What day the genial Angel to our sire
Brought her, in naked beauty more adorned,
More lovely, than Pandora, whom the gods
Endowed with all their gifts.

• • •

    Thus at their shady lodge arrived, both stood,
Both turned, and under open sky adored
The God that made both Sky, Air, Earth, and Heaven,
Which they beheld, the Moon's resplendent globe,
And starry Pole: "Thou also mad'st the Night,
Maker Omnipotent; and thou the Day,
Which we in our appointed work employed
Have finished happy in our mutual help
And mutual love, the crown of all our bliss
Ordained by thee; and this delicious place,
For us too large, where thy abundance wants
Partakers, and uncropt falls to the ground.
But thou hast promised from us two a race
To fill the Earth, who shall with us extol
Thy goodness infinite, both when we wake,
And when we seek, as now, thy gift of sleep."
    This said unanimous, and other rites
Observing none, but adoration pure,
Which God likes best, into their inmost bower
Handed they went; and, eased the putting-off
These troublesome disguises which we wear,
Straight side by side were laid; nor turned, I ween,
Adam from his fair spouse, nor Eve the rites
Mysterious of connubial love refused:

JOHN MILTON

Whatever hypocrites austerely talk
Of purity, and place, and innocence,
Defaming as impure what God declares
Pure, and commands to some, leaves free to all.
Our Maker bids increase; who bids abstain
But our destroyer, foe to God and Man?
Hail, wedded Love, mysterious law, true source
Of human offspring, sole propriety
In Paradise of all things common else!
By thee adulterous lust was driven from men
Among the bestial herds to range; by thee,
Founded in reason, loyal, just, and pure,
Relations dear, and all the charities
Of father, son, and brother, first were known.
Far be it that I should write thee sin or blame,
Or think thee unbefitting holiest place,
Perpetual fountain of domestic sweets,
Whose bed is undefiled and chaste pronounced,
Present, or past, as saints and patriarchs used.
Here Love his golden shafts employs, here lights
His constant lamp, and waves his purple wings,
Reigns here and revels; not in the bought smile
Of harlots—loveless, joyless, unendeared,
Casual fruition; nor in court amours,
Mixed dance, or wanton mask, or midnight ball,
Or serenate, which the starved lover sings
To his proud fair, best quitted with disdain.
These, lulled by nightingales, embracing slept,
And on their naked limbs the flowery roof
Showered roses, which the morn repaired. Sleep on,
Blest pair! and, O! yet happiest, if ye seek
No happier state, and know to know no more!

* * *

Part III: Renaissance to 1900

ANNE BRADSTREET, c. 1612-1672

To My Dear and Loving Husband

If ever two were one, then surely we.
If ever man were lov'd by wife, then thee.
If ever wife was happy in a man,
Compare with me, ye women, if you can.
I prize thy love more than whole Mines of gold,
Or all the riches that the East doth hold.
My love is such that Rivers cannot quench,
Nor ought but love from thee give recompence.
Thy love is such I can no way repay;
The heavens reward thee manifold I pray.
Then while we live, in love lets so persever,
That when we live no more, we may live ever.

* * *

RICHARD CRASHAW, c. 1613-1649

On Marriage

I would be married, but I'd have no wife:
I would be married to a single life.

Epithalamium

Come, virgin tapers of pure wax,
   Made in the hive of Love, all white

As snow, and yet as cold, where lacks
   Hymen's holy holy heat and light;
     Where blooming kisses
        Their beds yet keep
     And steep their blisses
        In rosy sleep;
Where sister buds yet wanting brothers
Kiss their own lips in lieu of others;
Help me to mourn a matchless maidenhead
        That now is dead.

A fine, thin negative thing it was,
   A nothing with a dainty name
Which pruned her plumes in Self-Love's glass
   Made up of fancy and fond fame;
     Within the shade
        Of its own wing
     It sat and played
        A self-crowned king;
A froward flower whose peevish pride
Within itself itself did hide,
Flying all fingers, and even thinking much
        Of its own touch.

This bird indeed the phoenix was
   Late chased by Love's revengeful arrows,
Whose wars now left the wonted pass
   As spared the little lives of sparrows
     To hunt this fool
        Whose froward pride
     Love's noble school
        And courts denied,
And froze the fruit of fair desire
Which flourisheth in mutual fire
'Gainst Nature, who 'mong all the webs she spun
        Ne'er wove a nun.

She, of Cupid's shafts afraid
   Left her own balm-breathing East,
And in a western bosom made
   A softer and a sweeter nest;
     There did she rest
       In the sweet shade
     Of a soft breast
       Whose beauties made
Thames oft stand still and lend a glass
While in her own she saw Heaven's face
And sent him full of her fair name's report
       To Thetis' court.

And now poor Love was at a stand:
   The crystal castle which she kept
Was proof against the proudest hand;
   There in safest hold she slept;
     His shafts' expense
       Left there no smart,
     But bounding thence
       Broached his own heart;
At length a fort he did devise
Built in noble Brampston's eyes,
And aiming thence, this matchless maidenhead
       Was soon found dead.

Yet Love in death did wait upon her
   Granting leave she should expire
In her fumes and have the honour
   T'exhale in flames of his own fire,
     Her funeral pile
       The marriage bed;
     In a sighed smile
       She vanished.
So rich a dress of death ne'er famed

The cradles where her kindred flamed;
So sweet her mother-phoenixes of the East
    Ne'er spiced their nest.

With many pretty, peevish trials
   Of angry yielding, faint denyings,
Melting Noes and mild denials,
   Dying lives and short-lived dyings,
     With doubtful eyes,
       Half smiles, half tears;
     With trembling joys
       And jocund fears,
Twixt the pretty twilight strife
Of dying maid and dawning wife,
Twixt rain and sunshine, this sweet maidenhead
    Alas is dead.

Happy he whose wakeful joys
   Kept the prize of this rich loss;
Happy she whose watery eyes
   Kiss no worse a weeping cross;
     Thrice happy he
       Partakes her store
     Thrice happy she
       Hath still the more.
Think not sweet bride, that faint shower slakes
The fires he from thy fair eyes takes;
Thy drops are salt, and while they think to tame
    Sharpen his flame.

Blest bridegroom, ere the rain be laid,
   Use good weather while it proves;
Those drops that wash away the maid
   Shall water your warm-planted loves;
     Fair youth, make haste
       Ere it be dry:

The sweet brine taste
　　From her moist eye;
Thy lips will find such dew as this is
Best season for a lover's kisses;
And those thy morning stars will better please
　　Bathed in those seas.

Nor may thy vine, fair oak, embrace thee
　　With ivy arms and empty wishes,
But with full bosom interlace thee
　　And reach her clusters to thy kisses;
　　　Safe may she rest
　　　　Her laden boughs
　　　On thy firm breast
　　　　And fill thy vows
Up to the brim, till she make even
Their full tops with the fair-eyed heaven,
And heaven to gild those glorious heroes' birth
　　Stoop and kiss earth.

Long may this happy heaven-tied band
　　Exercise its most holy art,
Keeping her heart within his hand,
　　Keeping his hand upon her heart;
　　　But from her eyes
　　　　Feel he no charms;
　　　Find she no joy
　　　　But in his arms;
May each maintain a well-fledged nest
Of winged loves in either's breast;
Be each of them a mutual sacrifice
　　Of either's eyes.

May their whole life a sweet song prove
　　Set to two well-composed parts

By music's noblest master, Love,
  Played on the strings of both their hearts;
    Whose mutual sound
      May ever meet
    In a just round,
      Not short though sweet;
Long may heaven listen to the song
And think it short though it be long;
Oh, prove't a well-set song indeed, which shows
      Sweet'st in the close!

* * *

HENRY VAUGHAN, 1622-1695

To the Best and Most Accomplished Couple——

Blessings as rich and fragrant crown your heads
  As the mild heaven on roses sheds,
  When at their cheeks, like pearls, they wear
  The clouds that court them in a tear;
  And may they be fed from above
  By him which first ordained your love!

Fresh as the hours may all your pleasures be,
  And healthful as eternity!
  Sweet as the flowers' first breath, and close
  As th' unseen spreadings of the rose,
  When he unfolds his curtained head,
  And makes his bosom the sun's bed.

Soft as yourselves, run your whole lives, and clear
    As your own glass, or what shines there;
    Smooth as Heaven's face, and bright as he,
    When, without mask or tiffany:
    In all your time not one jar meet,
    But peace as silent as his feet.

Like the day's warmth may all your comforts be,
    Untoiled for, and serene as he;
    Yet free and full as is that sheaf
    Of sunbeams gilding every leaf,
    When now the tyrant heat expires,
    And his cooled looks breathe milder fires.

And as those parcelled glories he doth shed
    Are the fair issues of his head,
    Which, ne'er so distant, are soon known
    By th' heat and lustre for his own;
    So may each branch of yours we see
    Your copies and our wonders be!

And when no more on earth you must remain,
    Invited hence to Heaven again,
    Then may your virtuous virgin-flames
    Shine on those heirs of your fair names,
    And teach the world that mystery,
    Yourselves in your posterity!

So you to both worlds shall rich presents bring,
And gathered up to Heaven, leave here a Spring.

* * *

JOHN DRYDEN, 1631-1700

Song
From *Amboyna*

The day is come, I see it rise
Betwixt the bride and bridegroom's eyes;
That golden day they wished so long,
Love picked it out amidst the throng;
He destined to himself this sun,
And took the reins, and drove him on:
In his own beams he drest him bright,
Yet bid him bring a better night.

The day you wished arrived at last,
You wish as much that it were past;
One minute more, and night will hide
The bridegroom and the blushing bride.
The virgin now to bed does go:
Take care, O youth, she rise not so:
She pants and trembles at her doom,
And fears and wishes thou would'st come.

The bridegroom comes, he comes apace,
With love and fury in his face;
She shrinks away; he close pursues,
And prayers and threats at once does use.
She, softly sighing, begs delay
And, with her hand, puts his away;
Now out aloud for help she cries,
And now despairing shuts her eyes.

Song
From *Marriage-à-la-Mode*

Why should a foolish Marriage Vow
    Which long ago was made,
Oblige us to each other now
    When Passion is decay'd?
We lov'd, and we lov'd, as long as we cou'd,
    Till our love was lov'd out in us both:
But our Marriage is dead, when the Pleasure is fled:
    'Twas Pleasure first made it an Oath.

If I have Pleasures for a Friend,
    And farther love in store,
What wrong has he whose joys did end,
    And who cou'd give no more?
'Tis a madness that he
Should be jealous of me,
Or that I shou'd bar him of another:
For all we can gain,
Is to give our selves pain,
When neither can hinder the other.

* * *

ELKANAH SETTLE, 1648-1724

A Congratulatory Poem to the Honoured Edmund Morris, Esq., on His Happy Marriage
From *Thalia Triumphans*

ELKANAH SETTLE apparently began in the 1680's and continued for many years to write eulogistic poems for important occasions in the lives of distinguished persons—funerals, births, return from travel, recovery from sickness, and weddings. A typical binding, that for the wedding poem of Edmund Morris in 1721, is of red morocco, the cover displaying a large coat of arms with an elaborate border of gold, flowers, Cupids' heads, and flying angels blowing trumpets. Samuel Johnson was probably the first to point out (in *Idler*, No. 12) that Settle had a standing epithalamium "of which only the first and last leaves were varied occasionally, and the intermediate pages were, by general terms left applicable alike to every character." In his bibliography of Settle's works, F. C. Brown lists five epithalamia which are identical (except for title page and the page which treats of the couple's illustrious ancestry). The five are for the weddings of Westfield, Ironmonger, Drake, Watts, and Green. I have compared the Drake poem with three others that Brown does not list—Cobham, Littleton, and Morris—and find it identical with them also except for the pages cited and an occasional word that may have been altered by the printer. Settle's stock poem runs eight pages, including the cover. I shall spare the readers of the present collection, except for a few lines from the beginning and the end.

> When the *Great FOUNDER* this vast Pile began,
> And ended with his Sixth Day's Labour, MAN,
> His Greatest Work the *Last*; stampt in his Own
> *Bright* IMAGE, call'd to th' Universal Throne:
> Yes *Earth, Heav'n, Stars,* and *Sun,* the whole *wide Round*
> All built for *Him,* all to *his Service* bound,
> These humbler Glories in the Front appear,
> Whilst *MAN,* true *SOVERAIGN*-like, brought up the Reer.
>
> . . . . . .
>
> Now happy Sir, melt a long Life away,
> A Life but one continued Nuptial Day;
> Nay to be Happier still, live Sir, to see
> Ev'n your own founded Immortality,

Yes, live to see your fruitful Table spread,
With those sweet Pledges of the *Genial Bed*,
Copies that shall the *Original* renew,
And make the STOCK Immortal whence they grew.

* * *

LEON LICHFIELD, c. 1662

The Printer, to Her Majesty
From *Domiduca Oxoniensis*

THIS IS THE POEM which Oxford University's printer added to a volume of student poems honoring the marriage of Katharine of Portugal to Charles II. The printer pretends that his "stamps"—that is, the letters of his typefaces—have by their own volition arranged themselves in the words of the poem in order to pay tribute to the bride.

I thought I'd done, but that my Presse took't ill
To speak for others, for itself stand still:
Impatient, to your view that it had shown
So many borrowed words, none of its own.
At your arrival, can there aught be dumb?
All things their joys would utter when you come.
My stamps all move and of themselves to You,
Not taught by others, would say something too.
They join themselves, and several stations take,
Framing all words the alphabet can make,
(As atoms at the world's first rise did fall,
Some here, some there, to form this mighty All)
To speak the good You bring, but yet they find,
Something beyond their reach still left behind;

Sham'd with the bold design that drew them forth,
To think that words could comprehend Your worth,
They drop back to their cells, resolving there,
Their ink, as badge of sadness, they will wear.
Henceforth despairing, e'er again to frame,
So good a word as KATHARINA's name.
But ere they parted this they bid me say,
Never were stamps so well employed as they.

—Leon Lichfield,
Printer to the University

* * *

MATTHEW PRIOR, 1664-1721

To a Friend on His Nuptials

When Jove lay blest in his Alcmena's charms,
   Three nights in one he prest her in his arms;
The sun lay set, and conscious Nature strove
To shade her God, and to prolong his love.
   From that auspicious night Alcides came;
What less could rise from Jove, and such a dame?
   May this auspicious night with that compare,
Nor less the joys, nor less the rising heir;
He strong as Jove, she like Alcmena fair!

Part III: Renaissance to 1900

CHRISTOPHER SMART, 1722-1771

Epithalamium on a Late Happy Marriage

When *Hymen* once the mutual Bands has wove,
Exchanging Heart for Heart, and Love for Love,
The happy Pair, with mutual Bliss elate,
Own to be single's an imperfect State.
But when two Hearts united thus agree
With equal sense, and equal Constancy,
This, HAPPINESS, is thy extreamest Goal,
'Tis Marriage both of Body, and of Soul,
'Tis making Heav'n below with matchless Love,
And's a fair Step to reach the Heav'n above.

* * *

WILLIAM BLAKE, 1757-1827

To the Evening Star
From *Poetical Sketches*

Thou fair-hair'd angel of the evening,
Now, whilst the sun rests on the mountains, light
Thy bright torch of love; thy radiant crown
Put on, and smile upon our evening bed!
Smile on our loves, and, while thou drawest the
Blue curtains of the sky, scatter thy silver dew

On every flower that shuts its sweet eyes
In timely sleep. Let thy west wind sleep on
The lake; speak silence with thy glimmering eyes,
And wash the dusk with silver. Soon, full soon,
Dost thou withdraw; then the wolf rages wide,
And the lion glares thro' the dun forest:
The fleeces of our flocks are cover'd with
Thy sacred dew: protect them with thine influence.

The Marriage Ring
From the Rossetti and Pickering Manuscripts

"Come hither my sparrows,
My little arrows.
If a tear or a smile
Will a man beguile,
If an amorous delay
Clouds a sunshiny day,
If the step of a foot
Smites the heart to its root,
'Tis the marriage ring
Makes each fairy a king."

So a fairy sung.
From the leaves I sprung.
He leap'd from the spray
To flee away.
But in my hat caught
He soon shall be taught.
Let him laugh, let him cry,
He's my butterfly;
For I've pull'd out the sting
Of the marriage ring.

Part III: Renaissance to 1900

To My Mirtle

To a lovely mirtle bound,
Blossoms show'ring all around,
O, how sick & weary I
Underneath my mirtle lie.
Why should I be bound to thee,
O, my lovely mirtle tree?

Eternity

He who binds to himself a joy
Does the winged life destroy;
But he who kisses the joy as it flies
Lives in eternity's sun rise.

* * *

WILLIAM WORDSWORTH, 1770-1850

Composed on the Eve of the Marriage of a Friend in the Vale of Grasmere

What need of clamorous bells, or ribands gay,
These humble Nuptials to proclaim or grace?
Angels of Love, look down upon the place,
Shed on the chosen Vale a sun-bright day!
Yet no proud gladness would the Bride display
Even for such promise:—serious is her face,

Modest her mien; and she, whose thoughts keep pace
With gentleness, in that becoming way
Will thank you. Faultless does the Maid appear;
No disproportion in her soul, no strife:
But, when the closer view of wedded life
Hath shown that nothing human can be clear
From frailty, for that insight may the Wife
To her indulgent Lord become more dear.

* * *

PERCY BYSSHE SHELLEY, 1792-1822

A Bridal Song

BOYS SING

Night! with all thine eyes look down!
    Darkness! weep thy holiest dew!
Never smiled the inconstant moon
    On a pair so true.

Haste, coy hour! and quench all light,
Lest eyes see their own delight!
Haste, swift hour! and thy loved flight
    Oft renew!

GIRLS SING

Fairies, sprites, and angels, keep her!
    Holy stars! permit no wrong!
And return to wake the sleeper,
    Dawn, ere it be long!
O joy! O fear! there is not one

Of us can guess what may be done
In the absence of the sun:—
　　Come along!

BOYS

Oh, linger long, thou envious eastern lamp
　　In the damp
　　　　Caves of the deep!

GIRLS

Nay, return, Vesper! urge the lazy car!
　　Swift unbar
　　　　The gates of Sleep!

CHORUS

The golden gate of Sleep unbar,
　　When Strength and Beauty, met together,
Kindle their image, like a star
　　In a sea of glassy weather.
May the purple mist of love
Round them rise, and with them move,
Nourishing each tender gem
Which, like flowers, will burst from them.
As the fruit is to the tree
May their children ever be!

Epithalamium for Charlotte Corday and Francis Ravaillac

IRONIC USE of the nuptial genre is demonstrated in this extract from a fragmentary work. Charlotte Corday was guillotined on July 17, 1793, for having murdered Marat by pulling from her bosom a dinner knife and plunging it into his left side.

T'is midnight now—athwart the murky air
    Dank lurid meteors shoot a livid gleam;
From the dark storm-clouds flashes a fearful glare
    It shows the bending oak, the roaring stream.
I pondered on the woes of lost mankind,
    I pondered on the ceaseless rage of kings;
My rapt soul dwelt upon the ties that bind
    The mazy volume of commingling things,
When fell and wild misrule to man stern sorrow brings.

. . . . .

Congenial minds will seek their kindred soul,
    E'en though the tide of time has rolled between;
They mock weak matter's impotent control,
    And seek of endless life the eternal scene.
At death's vain summons *this* will never die,
    In Nature's chaos *this* will not decay.
These are the bands which closely, warmly, tie
    Thy soul, O Charlotte, 'yond this chain of clay,
To him who thine must be till time shall fade away.

Yes, Francis! thine was the dear knife that tore
    A tyrant's heartstrings from his guilty breast;
Thine was the daring at a tyrant's gore
    To smile in triumph, to contemn the rest;
And thine, loved glory of thy sex! to tear
    From its base shrine a despot's haughty soul,
To laugh at sorrow in secure despair,
    To mock, with smiles, life's lingering control,
And triumph mid the griefs that round thy fate did roll.

Yes! the fierce spirits of the avenging deep
    With endless tortures goad their guilty shades.

I see the lank and ghastly spectres sweep
    Along the burning length of yon arcades;
And I see Satan stalk athwart the plain—
    He hastes along the burning soil of hell;
"Welcome, thou despots, to my dark domain!
With maddening joy mine anguished senses swell
To welcome to their home the friends I love so well."

. . . . . .

Hark! to those notes, how sweet, how thrilling sweet
They echo to the sound of angels' feet.

. . . . . .

Oh, haste to the bower where roses are spread,
For there is prepared thy nuptial bed.

* * *

ANONYMOUS, 1840

Fairy Chorus
From *The Bride's Marriage-Cake*

THE WEDDING CAKE for Queen Victoria and Prince Albert weighed nearly three hundred pounds and was more than nine feet in circumference and sixteen inches high. Atop the main plateau of the cake was a decorative superstructure consisting of two pedestals, the upper one supporting another plateau topped by the imposing figure of the goddess Minerva in the costume of ancient Rome but with the trident and spear of Britannia, her hands raised in blessing over the figures of the bride and groom, each about eleven inches tall. At the feet of the bridegroom was the figure of a dog, to denote fidelity, and at the feet of the Queen, a pair of turtledoves, to denote the felicities of the marriage state. Around the base of the dais on which the bridal couple

ANONYMOUS

joined hands were three little couples of Cupids and Psyches, one pair bearing a rose, another a shamrock, and the third a thistle. Another Cupid with a large book spread open in front of him was writing the date of the wedding, February 10, 1840. Still other Cupids played among the surrounding garlands of white flowers and white satin ribbons tied in lovers' knots. The cake was the work of Mr. J. C. Mawditt, the yeoman confectioner of the Royal Household.

An anonymous poet fancifully describes the preparation of the cake by Yeoman Mawditt and thousands of tiny helpers, creatures of a fairy-tribe, who hasten on glistening wings from the ends of the earth, singing and bearing sweets.

This nineteenth-century poem reminds us of one written more than two centuries earlier, Michael Drayton's "Prothalamion" from the eighth Nymphall of *The Muses Elizium*, in which another chorus of dainty fairies performs similar festive chores for one of their number (see p. 127).

In the twentieth century, the decoration of a bridal cake inspired E. E. Cummings to write a very different sort of poem (see p. 268).

>From the ends of the earth, from the ends of the earth,
Where the citrons are gold and the guava has birth,
Where the almond-boughs shed their soft blooms on the
    breeze,
And the lordliest fruitage emblazons the trees,
We have run—we have ridden—on winds vast and fleet,
To arrive in fit time with our treasure-loads sweet,
That shall powerfullest heighten, and heavenliest make
That glory of glories—the Bride's Marriage-Cake!

We have searched out the sweet from its innermost
    fold—
We've the orange-groves robbed of their ruddiest gold;
Our raisins we've chose from the vine's sweetest clusters,
Which imbibed, as they dried, the sun's virtues and lustres.
We've the sweetest of spices to worthily make,
That glory of glories—the Bride's Marriage-Cake.

Nor stay we—but, one and all, valiantly fling
In a glorious heap whatsoe'er he may bring:—
Be it sugars, or citrons, or perfumes, or spice,
Whatsoever is lusciously, fragrantly nice,
All to quickly compound, and triumphantly make,
That glory of glories—the Bride's Marriage-Cake.

* * *

ALFRED LORD TENNYSON, 1809-1892

From "*In Memoriam A. H. H.*"

O true and tried, so well and long,
    Demand not thou a marriage lay;
    In that it is thy marriage day
Is music more than any song.

Nor have I felt so much of bliss
    Since first he told me that he loved
    A daughter of our house; nor proved
Since that dark day a day like this;

Tho' I since then have number'd o'er
    Some thrice three years: they went and came,
    Remade the blood and changed the frame,
And yet is love not less, but more;

No longer caring to embalm
    In dying songs a dead regret,
    But like a statue solid-set,
And moulded in colossal calm.

ALFRED LORD TENNYSON

Regret is dead, but love is more
    Than in the summers that are flown,
    For I myself with these have grown
To something greater than before;

Which makes appear the songs I made
    As echoes out of weaker times,
    As half but idle brawling rhymes,
The sport of random sun and shade.

But where is she, the bridal flower,
    That must be made a wife ere noon?
    She enters, glowing like the moon
Of Eden on its bridal bower:

On me she bends her blissful eyes
    And then on thee; they meet thy look
    And brighten like the star that shook
Betwixt the palms of paradise.

O when her life was yet in bud,
    He too foretold the perfect rose.
    For thee she grew, for thee she grows
For ever, and as fair as good.

And thou art worthy; full of power;
    As gentle; liberal-minded, great,
    Consistent; wearing all that weight
Of learning lightly like a flower.

But now set out: the noon is near,
    And I must give away the bride;
    She fears not, or with thee beside
And me behind her will not fear:

For I that danced her on my knee,
    That watch'd her on her nurse's arm,
    That shielded all her life from harm
At last must part with her to thee;

Now waiting to be made a wife,
    Her feet, my darling, on the dead;
    Their pensive tablets round her head,
And the most living words of life

Breathed in her ear. The ring is on,
    The 'wilt thou' answer'd, and again
    The 'wilt thou' ask'd, till out of twain
Her sweet 'I will' has made you one.

Now sign your names, which shall be read,
    Mute symbols of a joyful morn,
    By village eyes as yet unborn;
The names are sign'd, and overhead

Begins the clash and clang that tells
    The joy to every wandering breeze;
    The blind wall rocks, and on the trees
The dead leaf trembles to the bells.

O happy hour, and happier hours
    Await them. Many a merry face
    Salutes them—maidens of the place,
That pelt us in the porch with flowers.

O happy hour, behold the bride
    With him to whom her hand I gave.
    They leave the porch, they pass the grave
That has to-day its sunny side.

ALFRED LORD TENNYSON

To-day the grave is bright for me,
    For them the light of life increased,
    Who stay to share the morning feast,
Who rest to-night beside the sea.

Let all my genial spirits advance
    To meet and greet a whiter sun;
    My drooping memory will not shun
The foaming grape of eastern France.

It circles round, and fancy plays,
    And hearts are warm'd and faces bloom,
    As drinking health to bride and groom
We wish them store of happy days.

Nor count me all to blame if I
    Conjecture of a stiller guest,
    Perchance, perchance, among the rest,
And, tho' in silence, wishing joy.

But they must go, the time draws on,
    And those white-favour'd horses wait;
    They rise, but linger; it is late;
Farewell, we kiss, and they are gone.

A shade falls on us like the dark
    From little cloudlets on the grass,
    But sweeps away as out we pass
To range the woods, to roam the park,

Discussing how their courtship grew,
    And talk of others that are wed,
    And how she look'd and what he said,
And back we come at fall of dew.

Again the feast, the speech, the glee,
    The shade of passing thought, the wealth
    Of words and wit, the double health,
The crowning cup, the three-times-three,

And last the dance;—till I retire:
    Dumb is that tower which spake so loud,
    And high in heaven the streaming cloud,
And on the downs a rising fire:

And rise, O moon, from yonder down,
    Till over down and over dale
    All night the shining vapour sail
And pass the silent-lighted town,

The white-faced halls, the glancing rills,
    And catch at every mountain head,
    And o'er the friths that branch and spread
Their sleeping silver thro' the hills;

And touch with shade the bridal doors,
    With tender gloom the roof, the wall;
    And breaking let the splendour fall
To spangle all the happy shores

By which they rest, and ocean sounds,
    And, star and system rolling past,
    A soul shall draw from out the vast
And strike his being into bounds,

And, moved thro' life of lower phase,
    Result in man, be born and think,
    And act and love, a closer link
Betwixt us and the crowning race

Of those that, eye to eye, shall look
    On knowledge; under whose command
    Is Earth and Earth's, and in their hand
Is Nature like an open book;

No longer half-akin to brute,
    For all we thought and loved and did,
    And hoped, and suffer'd, is but seed
Of what in them is flower and fruit;

Whereof the man, that with me trod
    This planet, was a noble type
    Appearing ere the times were ripe,
That friend of mine who lives in God,

That God, which ever lives and loves,
    One God, one law, one element,
    And one far-off divine event,
To which the whole creation moves.

*   *   *

GERARD MANLEY HOPKINS, 1844-1889

At the Wedding March

God with honour hang your head,
Groom, and grace you, bride, your bed
With lissome scions, sweet scions,
Out of hallowed bodies bred.

Each be other's comfort kind:
Déep, déeper than divined,
Divine charity, dear charity,
Fast you ever, fast bind.

Then let the March tread our ears:
I to him turn with tears
Who to wedlock, his wonder wedlock,
Déals tríumph and immortal years.

Epithalamion

ONE OF THE Jesuit priest's last poems was an unfinished ode written in 1888 for the marriage of his brother, Everard. Father Hopkins may have worked on the poem while supervising an examination, for the fragmentary manuscript consists of four sides of penciled rough sketches, and five sides of quarto first draft, on "Royal University of Ireland" candidates' paper.

Hark, hearer, hear what I do; lend a thought now, make believe
We are leafwhelmed somewhere with the hood
Of some branchy bunchy bushybowered wood,
Southern dean or Lancashire clough or Devon cleave,
That leans along the loins of hills, where a candy-
    coloured, where a gluegold-brown
Marbled river, boisterously beautiful, between
Roots and rocks is danced and dandled, all in froth and
    water-blowballs, down.
We are there, when we hear a shout
That the hanging honeysuck, the dogeared hazels in the cover
Makes dither, makes hover
And the riot of a rout
Of, it must be, boys from the town
Bathing: it is summer's sovereign good.

By there comes a listless stranger: beckoned by the noise
He drops towards the river: unseen
Sees the bevy of them, how the boys
With dare and with downdolphinry and bellbright bod-
    ies huddling out,
Are earthworld, airworld, waterworld thorough hurled,
    all by turn and turn about.

This garland of their gambol flashes in his breast
Into such a sudden zest
Of summertime joys
That he hies to a pool neighbouring; sees it is the best
There; sweetest, freshest, shadowiest;
Fairyland; silk-beech, scrolled ash, packed sycamore,
    wild wychelm, hornbeam fretty overstood
By. Rafts and rafts of flake leaves light, dealt so, painted
    on the air,
Hang as still as hawk or hawkmoth, as the stars or as the
    angels there,
Like the thing that never knew the earth, never off roots
Rose. Here he feasts: lovely all is! No more: off with—
    down he dings
His bleachèd both and woolwoven wear:
Careless these in coloured wisp
All lie tumbled-to; then with loop-locks
Forward falling, forehead frowning, lips crisp
Over finger-teasing task, his twiny boots
Fast he opens, last he off wrings
Till walk the world he can with bare his feet
And come where lies a coffer, burly all of blocks
Built of chancequarrièd, selfquainèd, hoar-huskèd rocks
And the water warbles over into, filleted with glassy
    grassy quicksilvery shivès and shoots
And with heavenfallen freshness down from moorland
    still brims,

(199)

Dark or daylight on and on. Here he will then, here he
    will the fleet
Flinty kindcold element let break across his limbs
Long. Where we leave him, froliclavish, while he looks
    about him, laughs, swims.

Enough now; since the sacred matter that I mean
I should be wronging longer leaving it to float
Upon this only gambolling and echoing-of-earth note—

What is . . . . .the delightful dean?
Wedlock. What the water? Spousal love.
. . . .
. . . .
                                                                   turns
Father, mother, brothers, sisters, friends
Into fairy trees, wildflowers, woodferns
Rankèd round the bower
. . . .

European

CLÉMENT MAROT, 1496-1544
Translated from the French by Cécile Schreiber and Virginia Tufte

Toast to a Departing Duchess

In 1528 when Princess Renée of France went to Italy as bride of the Duke of Ferrara, Marot wrote a wedding song. Most of the nine stanzas are adapted from Catullus's Carmen 62, but the last stanza, translated below, is novel.

>Alas, dear duchess,
>>What do you do?
>>For one prince's love,
>>You leave a whole nation
>>That long has loved you.
>
>We can only be sad
>>But your new land rejoices—
>>There a new Arch of Triumph
>>And a great theater resound
>>With welcoming voices.
>
>Go then, dear duchess,
>>To your new duke's court—
>>And may the belt of your gown
>>Soon be too short.

Part III: Renaissance to 1900

PIERRE DE RONSARD, 1524-1585

Translated from the French by Cécile Schreiber and Virginia Tufte

The Wager

From *Pastoral Song for the Nuptials of Charles, Duke of Lorraine, and Claude, Daughter of the King*

AMONG PASTORAL wedding songs, a form much in vogue in sixteenth-century France, one of the most ingenious is a 500-line poem written in 1559 by Pierre de Ronsard. The poem includes a singing match between two shepherds, Perot (representing Ronsard himself) and Bellot (representing his friend and fellow-poet, Joachim du Bellay). Judge of the contest is Michau (Michel de l'Hospital). Other poets mentioned in the extract which follows are Thony (Antoine de Bäif) and Remy (Remy Belleau). Ronsard's poem is written entirely in rhymed Alexandrine couplets, with the caesura skillfully varied. In the excerpt that follows (titled "The Wager" by the translators), the two shepherds, Perot and Bellot, set up a wager and hold a contest to see who can compose the better wedding song. Parts of the matching songs and the judge's decision are translated here. The reader will hear echoes of Theocritus and Catullus.

BELLOT

For your music, Perot, all the shepherds have praise,
You're the best on the flute in a half-dozen ways,
But when they say your skill equals mine I am shaken;
I'd like to show you that they are mistaken.
And so I've been wishing I'd run into you
For here is the thing I've been wanting to do—
It's to try against yours my musical skill,
To place a great peak beside a small hill.

PEROT

Though you come to confront me so boldly, my friend,
To such great bravado I'll soon make an end.
So let's have a wager. Now as for me,
What shall I bet, what shall it be?
I know, I'll put up a bird cage I made
The other day as I sat in the shade
Watching my cows with my good friend Thony—
He's a better singer than we'll ever be.

The bars I made of some tea herbs I picked,
And the tiny white perch, of a hazelnut stick.
From thin skins of reeds I have woven the floor,
And here in the corner—one of the four—
I have hung the shell of a snail by a hair,
You'd think that the snail himself built it there.

Through here I have hollowed a tunnel, quite clean,
And the small posts of the building stand in between,
Cut from blackberry stem as thin as can be,
And this woven rope Remy gave to me.
I like the colors because they're so gay.
Remy won it, he said, from Thony one day.

In the cage I have prisoned a young lark, pretty bird,
Whose song is the sprightliest you've ever heard.
Cassandra my sweet tried to get it from me
For a fat calf and a kid. 'Twas no use as you see.
However, it's yours if you win from me now,
But it will take a good song to force me to bow.

BELLOT

To match the cage and the bird, what stake shall I
    choose?
I'll wager my basket. To weave it I've used
Little branches of water willow, tiny at the base,

And larger at the top; see how finely they're laced.
The handle's from a holly—here's how you bend it—
I cut my finger with my scythe when I thinned it.
And I shouldn't tell you, but the pain's still acute
In my poor cut finger when I try my flute.

I've painted on my basket, though it's small in size,
Mercury and Io and the hundred eyes
Of Argus—Argus, the poor shepherd lad
Whom Mercury killed. Here you see him after he's had
His head cut off. From his blood a peacock springs
With a hundred eyes on its tail and its wings.

I use the basket to carry strawberries, roses and such
To the market. My Olive likes it so much
She tried to trade me her dog, which I wouldn't take,
But now this fine basket I put up as a stake.
It's worth as much as your bird and cage, you'll agree,
But who will judge us? Who'll referee?
Do you see that old shepherd who is coming there
With the venerable beard and honored grey hair
And crook in his hand, made of firm knotty wood,
And jacket of deerskin? Let's ask this good
man. He's greatly revered for the knowledge he wields,
By all the French shepherds who come to these fields.

PEROT

I know him, Bellot, and I've long heard him sing.
With tributes to him the pastures still ring,
And once, proud to say, this great singer deigned
To praise my humble songs to Charlot of Lorraine.

MICHAU

What are you saying, children dear to the Muse?
The woods here are green and the flowers profuse.

PIERRE DE RONSARD

Here all the lands are walled by small mountains,
From all sides rivulets murmur, and fountains.
You should not be idle, my children, but sing
Not of playful romance but more beautiful thing.
Your spirits will rise, for there's sweet work to do
On a song that will live long after you.

Have you not heard that the great god Pan,
God of shepherd, and admired of man,
Today grants his beautiful daughter Claudine
To the worthy young shepherd, Charlot of Lorraine? . . .

To celebrate the wedding there will be a great feast
And dancing from evening to morning at least
With the gods of the forest, the nymphs and dryads,
Fauns, oreads, satyrs, Pan himself, and the naiads. . . .

Your musettes must explode with the sacred good fate
Of this prince of Lorraine and his beautiful mate.
Bellot, go ahead, let your best skills be tried,
You will sing of the groom, Perot of the bride.
It's better, my children, to salute this great day
Than to wear out your flute on love song and play.

BELLOT

Oh, God of weddings, Hymen, Hymenee,
Put on ensaffroned coat, and then I pray,
Encase your feet in slippers blue, and please
Take up your flaming torch. Then you must sneeze
Three times, and three times more then give the sign
That Claudine and Charlot, princes divine,
May be forever blessed. And bring with you
The holy Cyprienne. And summon too
 Cupid her son, his bow and arrows in hand,
To work his wiles on eyes of this young man.
This child-groom from Lorraine though young's not one

(205)

With two or three small goats asleep in sun,
But herds of oxen, ewes, and cows as well
In grassy vales of Meuse and blue Moselle,
Spreading to Bar and over grassy plain
And mountain sides in all of fair Lorraine.

In grace and beauty this young bridegroom stands
Above the shepherds of all other lands
Like fine young bull above the cows nearby
Or towering cypress reaching huge and high
Above a little copse, or like tall reed
Dwarfing the grassy streamside's lowly weed.
A silky curling beard adorns His Grace,
Blonde complement to his Adonis-face;
His forehead is the dawn, and starry skies
Relieve the dark with light from his fine eyes.

Besides all these, his skill at sports I sing,
Jumping, jousting, throwing darts or sling,
And by rough blows he rescues from wolf's throat
And takes back to its dam a trembling goat. . . .
Shepherds, give shade to sacred springs, and shower
Along the paths the fair and purple flower.
Swell the bagpipes with various rhyme and song
For Vesper brings night soon, though it seems long.
Sun, hasten your chariot, shorten your stay.
Charlot likes the night much better than the day.

Thus Bellot concludes his sweet song with dispatch,
And sprightly Perot takes his turn in the match.

PEROT

Oh, Juno Lucina, you who preside
Over wedding and household, you who guide
Your peacock-coupled car as swift as wind
Across the width of heaven to earth's end,

Come, bring your kindly daughter, and I pray
Cast favor on our Claudine's wedding day.
As in early morning the beautiful rose
Honors the garden wherein it grows,
The princess Claudine is the honor of all
The shepherdesses, surpassing them like tall
And regal pine above the waving fern.
No one knows better how to shape and turn
The flowers into chaplets for fair hair.
Or how to bind the rose and lily there.
With gold and silken thread and subtle skill
Her needle draws designs none can excel.

I see here in these woods two turtledoves
Who constantly caress. As these young loves
Shall long abide in amorous repose,
May you Claudine so live with Charles your spouse.
Into my pretty basket I shall reap
Sweet flowers from the banks to make a heap
Of petals round about the bridal pair,
While genial song shall fill the blithesome air.
So happy a girl has a happy mother
And father, too, and a happy brother
But the happiness of all these is mild
Compared to his who begets her child. . . .

A hundred and a hundred joys this night
Await the two now linked by wedding rite.
Kisses will shower on forehead and hand;
Their number will be like the grains of sand
Or the blades of grass that cover the plain.
Such is the tally of sweets lovers gain. . . .
Now Vesper announces the shadows of night.
Vine marries elm in Star's nuptial light. . . .
Partake of youth's pastimes, for age soon will wither.
May a child bless each year of your lives together.

Thus with his oaten pipe, the good Perot concludes,
His echoing song redoubled by the murmuring woods.
Then Michau leaped up to express his great pleasure
And to praise the two shepherds in equal measure.

MICHAU

Your harmony, children, is as sweet and saucy
As the singing stream's notes on the mossy
Rocks, or the voice of the swan or nightingale
Rejoicing in April's new wooded vale.
May your two mouths be filled ever, my friends,
With manna, your hats with roses, and your hands
With sweet marjoram. You play equally well
On your flutes. Who is better? I cannot tell.
To settle your bet, just exchange your wage—
Perot, take his basket, and you Bellot, his cage.
Now return, my children, to your pastures green
And your fellow shepherds. May your life be serene.

* * *

GASPAR GIL POLO, c. 1530-1591

Translated from the Spanish by Bartholomew Young (about 1580)

Ring Forth, Fair Nymphs, Your Joyful Songs for Gladness

Carol for Joy of the New Marriage between Sirenus and Diana
From *Diana Enamorada*

Let now each mead with flowers be depainted,
  Of sundry colours, sweetest odours glowing;
Roses yield forth your smells so finely tainted;
  Calm winds the green leaves move with gentle blowing.

>   The crystal rivers flowing
>   With waters be increased;
>   And since each one from sorrow now hath ceased,
>   From mournful plaints and sadness,
>   Ring forth, fair nymphs, your joyful songs for gladness!

> Let springs and meads all kind of sorrow banish,
>   And mournful hearts the tears that they are bleeding;
> Let gloomy clouds with shining morning vanish;
>   Let every bird rejoice that now is breeding.
>   And since, by new proceeding,
>   With marriage now obtained,
>   A great content by great contempt is gained,
>   And you devoid of sadness:
>   Ring forth, fair nymphs, your joyful songs for gladness!

> Who can make us to change our firm desires,
>   And soul to leave her strong determination,
> And make us freeze in ice, and melt in fires,
>   And nicest hearts to love with emulation?
>   Who rids us from vexation,
>   And all our minds commandeth,
>   But great Felicia, that his might withstandeth
>   That filled our hearts with sadness?
>   Ring forth, fair nymphs, your joyful songs for gladness!

> Your fields with their distilling favours cumber,
>   Bridegroom and happy bride, each heavenly power!
> Your flocks, with double lambs increased in number,
>   May never taste unsavoury grass and sour!
>   The winter's frost and shower
>   Your kids, your pretty pleasure,
>   May never hurt! and blest with so much treasure,

> To drive away all sadness,
> Ring forth, fair nymphs, your joyful songs for
>   gladness!

Of that sweet joy delight you with such measure,
   Between you both fair issue to engender;
Longer than Nestor may you live in pleasure;
   The gods to you such sweet content surrender,
      That may make mild and tender
      The beasts in every mountain,
      And glad the fields and woods and every fountain,
      Abjuring former sadness,
      Ring forth, fair nymphs, your joyful songs for
        gladness!

Let amorous birds with sweetest notes delight you;
   Let gentle winds refresh you with their blowing;
Let fields and forests with their good requite you,
   And Flora deck the ground where you are going,
      Roses and violets strowing,
      The jasmine and the gillyflower
      With many more; and never in your bower
      To taste of household sadness.
      Ring forth, fair nymphs, your joyful songs for
        gladness!

Concord and peace hold you for aye contented,
   And in your joyful state live you so quiet,
That with the plague of jealousy tormented
   You may not be, nor fed with Fortune's diet;
      And that your names may fly yet
      To hills unknown with glory.
      But now, because my breast, so hoarse and sorry
      It faints, may rest from singing,
      End nymphs, your songs, that in the clouds are
        ringing.

TORQUATO TASSO, 1544-1595
Translated from the Italian by David Rafael Wang

To the Father of the Bride

Fortunate father, blessed ancestor,
When your beautiful Lucrezia is still young
And enraptured with her girlish beauty
Is her beloved spouse, into her happy state
Is born Laura, the child, who comes at the time
Like the rose in green hedgerow before the dawn
Or the perfumed branch in a tender plant;
And, happy, you welcome her in your arms
And lovingly look at her beautiful eyes,
Her forehead, and those tresses that will become
Golden and long. Thus, dear Alexander,
May your offspring always flower and thrive,
And in your seeds may live your name, and in each
A renewal be given to your life.

*   *   *

PIERRE POUPO, c. 1552-1591
Translated from the French by Cécile Schreiber and Virginia Tufte

Prayers of a Christian Bridegroom

I

Dear Lord, if ever I might hope for grace,
If I might ask of you the highest gift,

And if you are indeed all-perfect, Father,
If such be true, Lord, make me feel your might.
   Tighten, tie, entwine, link, glue, incorporate
Phyllis's heart and mine with cord so strong
That accident or unrelenting shears
Of death himself can never break it.
   By nature a father does not give his child
Who asks for an egg a snake instead,
So grant, please, my desire and better still,
   Make inner selves excel the outer
That mind may honor body's beauty,
Pure stone honoring the ring which gilds it.

II

   I request of you, Lord, an immense favor,
I'm asking for Phyllis, pearl without peer,
But if I sought from you some smaller gift,
Would I not be misjudging your munificence?
   I know full well my weakness and unworth
But having seen the joy of those you bless,
Those whom you freely give your infinite boon,
Even I dare to hope against all hope.
   Give her to me, Lord. Say the good word,
And by some happy sign bestow new life
On heart long held abject before Fear's sword.
   I hear your answer Lord. I feel soul's leap.
God has said yes, my love. Now you must speak.
I know you will not contradict your Father.

III

   If to thank you, God, for your great favor,
I sacrificed a thousand cattle of praise,
Would that not be, Oh Lord, only a drop
In exchange for an ocean of blessings?

The most beautiful and best of what is yours
Under the spacious azure of the skies,
You have given to me, Oh gracious God,
In her angel face and heavenly spirit.

Nor eye, nor ear, nor tongue of mortal man
Can see, or hear or speak the slightest part
Of the blessed peace you grant your own.

A good marriage is an approach to Heaven:
Man's earthly body makes him neighbor to Hell,
But he who is well married is near to Paradise.

* * *

LOPE DE VEGA CARPIO, 1562-1613
Translated from the Spanish

Song for the Divine Bride and Mother

Where are you going, shepherdess,
alone on the height?
But she who carries the sun
has no fear of night.

Where are you going, Mary,
bride and mother, too,
of the glorious God
who created you?

When day dies in the west
what will you do
if you're still in the woods
and the dark catches you?

Part III: Renaissance to 1900

> But she who carries the sun
> has no fear of night—
> to see by the stars vexes me
> but your eyes give forth light.
>
> Now the dark night catches the stars,
> stars turn pale at the wondrous sight,
> but she who carries the sun
> has no fear of night.

* * *

GIAMBATTISTA MARINO, 1569-1625
Translated from the Italian

The Bed

THE EXTRAVAGANT and sensuous imagery of *Il Letto (The Bed)* is characteristic of Marino's ten long epithalamia and, to a lesser degree, of other Italian wedding poems. The poem is built on a favorite theme of the Italians, the love battle in the nuptial chamber, a theme that had its origin in ritual and history.

The custom of exhibiting ceremonially the coverlet from the nuptial bed as evidence of the struggle and victory receives novel treatment in *Il Letto*, particularly in the last stanza, where the poet substitutes Cupid's blindfold for the bed cover.

> The midpoint is past
> In her dark journey,
> And in our hemisphere
> Night is rising to the highest point.

The archer-goddess
From the top of the sky
With arrows of silver wounds the dense veil
Of dark air,
Casting doubt as to moonlight or dawn.

How many soft lights
Noble and smiling
She burns on her roof,
As many as she has placed in the eternal temple,
Unhidden by shadow,
Their rays shining.
Never were unfurled in the eighth circle of the sky
More serene splendors,
More beautiful night for happier loves.

All now is silent,
The festive scene,
The dances and suppers
Where Mincio and Dora raised their horn.
And in the royal dwelling,
Rich and lofty,
The now sleepy pages and grooms have
Made dark as the grave
Each spent candle in tongs of silver.

In quiet repose
Among sheets soft and white
Lie languid and spent
Margherita and Francesco, the royal spouses,
In love's arena,
Fury abated,
Chaste contests resolved in caresses,
Retreats in advances,
Warring in peace, athletes unarmed.

Their battleground and their camp
Was a sweet chamber
Whose secret key was turned
By the faithful guardian, the winged archer.
Here against the well-born hero,
Forthright and courageous,
The lovely warrior had come forth to battle,
Her shield and armour
(Against tender blows) were her naked breasts.

High overhead
A great canopy
Curtained with Tyrian purple
Spread rich and royal shade for the sweet attack.
There embossed in enamel,
Ornate and treasured,
Were trophies of Emanuels and Gonzagas,
With topaz and peridot,
Polished and cut by dark Ethiopian hand.

Scattered about the soft bed
Were sweet perfumed spirits,
Arabian breaths,
Wafting throughout the noble canopy,
Signs of scented smoke,
Heavenward,
Vapors divine and ethereal,
Auras pure and light
Of Indian gums and Iberian mixtures.

With them, keeping vigil,
Next to rich feathers,
A pale candle quivers,
Small wavering fire in bracket of gold,

Seeming to say, I die,
I, lustful light, also die,
With you, I melt in the living flame,
But meanwhile drop by drop
Beautiful souls consume more living flame.

Beautiful souls,
Lovers and enemies,
Shyly proceed
In love's joyous battle, delighted palms
Provoking bodies
To innocent homicide,
Alternating among their sweet challenges
Biting and warm,
Breaths as trumpets, kisses as heralds.

Kisses rain in clusters,
Fall like thousand hailstones
Exploding uncounted,
As many as the sun has atoms, the fire has embers.
Love, like ivy or octopus,
Stronger and twice as tenacious,
Orders the knots and redoubles the blows
Of kisses without end,
Writing their number on the bed curtain.

Lips united
Send kisses to hearts.
Hearts, overflowing,
Draw from kisses the souls, overcome with love.
Souls, ravished by love,
Wander joyfully
To quench their thirst in the fount of delight;
There
Lips become breasts and sweetnesses milk.

Often kisses are forgotten
By the young man,
Musing in adoration of her beauty,
Gentle reflection of the beauty of God.
His desires halt
And he sighs, overcome
Like an eagle before the Sun, or butterfly in the Light;
He worships, and speaks silently,
I want to die, marveling, and to marvel, dying.

In the trembling zephyrs
Of the blessed lights,
The enamoured lights,
Turning at times in merciful round,
He recounts and marks
His happy martyrdoms,
And two tongues are joined into one,
Smiling small words
Often killed by kisses and sighs.

"Oh, celestial beauty,
Comfort of my griefs,
Sweet harbor
In the heavy tempests of love,
Are these the very limbs,
(Or do I dream or imagine?)
Are these the ones I love, these that I hold?
Of this untouched good
Am I today to become the happy possessor?"

"But who fights
And denies just requests?
Why do you not allow
Me to touch the last step of my hopes?

Why should we not
Pluck the flower
That in a short time will produce blooms
To fill Italy
And all the world with noble fruit?"

"If it is true
As my prophet Mantuan predicts,
If one can believe
What the heavens have promised,
From emulators of ancestors
Like ourselves,
From us will come a long line of heroes
Born to kingdoms
Ever increasing, a succession of pledges."

When she hears this speech,
The virgin's face is like
A fresh rose,
And as if she wished to hide,
Timid and blushing,
She lowers her eyes,
Answering only with tears,
Which little by little he tastes,
Two streams of water, an ocean of fire.

The nuptial couch,
Scene of the nightly diversions,
Is transformed by the flying Cupids
Into the kingdom and palace of Love.
The ingenious Cupids create
Pillows of roses
For the beautiful cheek of the damsel,
And make pillows of feathers
For the tired young man.

Thus do they contend
In close combat,
Falling back, attacking,
The beautiful warrior and her champion.
The match moves toward its end
Amid retreats and advances,
And with souls summoned for the final blows
In the love encounter,
One is hit in the breast, the other in the heart.

Conquered,
The unconquered falls,
And the wounder
Rests in battle, himself wounded.
In this great conflict
Hearts set free the senses.
Trembling and sighing, spirits faint,
Breathless,
And eyelids cease their motion.

Joyously hovering,
The souls of the lovers
Begin flight together
And through Love's doorway glimpse Heaven.
Dying a death
Of such sweet pleasure,
Each lover, equally blest,
Gazes at the other's face
And judges Paradise to be less beautiful.

Love, who forced the war
Each with the other,
Careful and very wise judge
Of the dubious contest, removes his blindfold
And at last sees the beautiful couple

SIMON DACH

Fatigued and disarmed.
In proper rite, Love anoints the blindfold
With red
Proof of virginity, emblem of victory.

* * *

From the Circle around SIMON DACH, 1605-1659
Translated from the German by Christa Wolf and Virginia Tufte

Anke von Tharau

Anke von Tharau's the one I adore,
She is my life and my gold and my store.

Anke von Tharau to me once again
Offers her heart both in love and in pain.

Anke von Tharau, my wealth and my goods,
You are my soul and my flesh and my blood.

Even through hail, bitter weather and rain
Ever together we two will remain.

Sickness, affliction, distresses and wrong
Tie the knot firmly and make our love strong.

Just as a palm tree grows higher and higher,
Thwarting attack both by wind and by fire,

So will affection continue to grow,
Love giving answer to suffering and woe.

Even if fortune decree we must part,
Taking you where no kind sun cheers the heart,

I'll trail you through forest and far ocean's damp,
Through ice, through iron, through enemy camp.

Anke von Tharau, my star and my sun,
Now and forever, our hearts become one.

* * *

JOHANN WOLFGANG VON GOETHE, 1749–1832

Translated from the German by Christa Wolf and Virginia Tufte

Wedding Song

In nuptial chamber far from feast
Devoted Cupid keeps the watch
Lest wanton friends contrive some jest
Against the waiting bridal couch.
He waits for you. The torch's whorls
Encircle him, and golden flames
Impel the incense-scented mist
About the room in sensuous curls.

Your heart pounds when the hour sounds
That chases festive noises home,
Your eyes caress the lovely mouth
Now ever yours and yours alone.
You leave and guests, exclaiming, leave:
"Such joy be also ours, we pray."
The mother cries, and ever strict
Would even now keep you away.

To enter bliss complete and true
Love's sanctuary beckons you.
The torch, the waiting Cupid tries
To calm to gentle lamp, then hies
To aid the bride's undressing.
Observing he's less deft than you,
He shyly turns and shields his eyes
And, smiling, gives his blessing.

* * *

CLEMENS BRENTANO, 1778-1842

Translated from the German by Christa Wolf and Virginia Tufte

Bridal Song

THE BRIDE'S FRIENDS

Come join us, come join us, beautiful bride,
No longer, dear friend, will you be at our side.
Your pretty veil's weighted by tears from sad eyes.
Oh, the beautiful bride, just see how she cries.
Now you must leave your sweet maiden life
For this is the day you become a wife.

Put on, put on, for a short short hour
Rich sparkling tokens, sweet silken flower.
Your pretty veil's weighted by tears from sad eyes.
Oh, the beautiful bride, just see how she cries.
Now you must cover these braids so fair,
Don yellow bonnet on golden hair.

Part III: Renaissance to 1900

Don't laugh, don't laugh, your slippers so light
Will pinch you, I'm sure, because they are tight.
Your pretty veil's weighted by tears from sad eyes,
Oh, the beautiful bride, just see how she cries.
Now when others go dancing, hand clasped in hand,
There by the cradle, you'll have to stand.

Wave your hand, wave your hand, now you can't linger,
For soon faithful ring will pinch the fair finger.
Your pretty veil's weighted by tears from sad eyes.
Oh, the beautiful bride, just see how she cries.
Today they look lovely, those shining new rings.
Tomorrow you'll feel that they've turned into chains.

Dance today, dance, your last dance on the heath,
When the roses have died, you'll find thorns in the wreath.
Your pretty veil's weighted by tears from sad eyes,
Oh, the beautiful bride, just see how she cries.
The fair flowering meadow now you must yield
To the new row you hoe in fresh greening field.

* * *

HEINRICH HEINE, 1797-1856

Translated from the German by Christa Wolf and Virginia Tufte

Knight Olaf

A KNIGHT is sentenced to die for having seduced the king's daughter, Heinrich Heine describes the couple's wedding day.

I

Outside the great cathedral door
Two red-clad figures stand,
The one a king, and at his call
A hangman, axe in hand.

The king commands the hangman,
"I hear the closing rite,
The nuptial mass is ending,
Make your good axe sharp and bright."

The bells ring out, the organ sounds,
Outside the people press.
A colorful and gay parade
Comes forth in festive dress.

The lovely bride is sad and grave,
As pale as death, her face,
But bold Sir Olaf's eyes are bright,
He smiles with lively grace.

He quickly turns to dark-faced king
And, smiling, dares to say,
"Good morning, father of my bride,
I know I die today.

That I must die I know, but, sir,
Till midnight let me stay
To celebrate with torch and dance
On this my wedding day.

I pray that I may live, my king,
Till wine has made its rounds,
Until the last dance has been danced,
And stroke of midnight sounds.

The king commands the hangman,
"Wait till twelve this night
To take the life of this bold prince.
Make your good axe sharp and bright."

II

Sir Olaf sits at wedding feast,
The last goblet he drains dry.
His young wife at his shoulder
Can only sigh—
And the hangman stands at the door.

The round dance begins and the knight joins hands
With his wife, and the music plays fast,
Madly they whirl by gleam of the torch,
The dance is his last—
And the hangman stands at the door.

The beautiful strings of the fiddles sing out,
The anxious flutes sigh, sadly afraid.
Wildly the dancers circle the floor—
Those who watch are dismayed—
And the hangman stands at the door.

The music echoes throughout the great hall,
The bride hears the whisper of lover so bold,
"My love for you is true and warm—
The grave is so cold"—
And the hangman stands at the door.

III

Sir Olaf, it is midnight now,
The price must now be paid,
For you seduced a royal child,
This fair and noble maid.

CONRAD FERDINAND MEYER

The monks are murmuring funeral prayer,
The man in red takes stock,
He stands prepared with polished axe
And waits at blackened block.

The knight descends to the court below
Which gleams with lights and swords,
He smiles and turns to waiting crowd
And, smiling, speaks these words:

"I bless the sun, I bless the moon,
The stars that cross the sky,
I also bless the little birds
That whistle from on high."

"I bless the sea, I bless the land,
The flowered lea where I have roved,
I bless the violets, gentle, sweet
As the eyes of my beloved."

"You, violet eyes of my sweet wife,
It is through you I lose my life!
I also bless the eldertree
Where you surrendered, dear, to me."

* * *

CONRAD FERDINAND MEYER, 1825-1898
Translated from the German by Christa Wolf and Virginia Tufte

Wedding Song

Out of the house and power of her parents
steps the timid bride

(227)

to the crossroads of life—
Go and love and suffer!

Momentarily free, again enyoked,
how the young heart beats
in silken dress—
Go and love and suffer!

The bright joy of pious eyes
outshines the flashing light
of heirloom gems adorning her full breast—
Go and love and suffer!

Mark it well, blonde-haired bride,
pain and joy are sister and brother,
the two inseparable.
Go and love and suffer!

Oriental

SEIKI FUJINO, *19th Century*
Translated from the Japanese by Sumako Kimizuka

Treasure Boat

AT JAPANESE wedding receptions, one of the guests will often begin to chant or recite a wedding poem and others will join in. This poem and the one that follows are among the familiar poems often heard at twentieth-century wedding receptions. The treasure boat is a symbol of happiness and prosperity. The seven deities are the gods who arrange weddings. In October—the month without deities—they are resting. In November they come forth, and November is the Japanese wedding month.

> The character "Treasure" written on the sail
>   can be seen in the distance.
> The sea is smooth and calm,
>   and the crimson sun shines brightly.
> The seven deities on board the ship
>   all are smiling.
> This is the ship of treasure,
>   laden with gold, silver, and jade.

Part III: Renaissance to 1900

TENRAI KONO, *19th Century*
Translated from the Japanese by Sumako Kimizuka

Wedding Celebration

The new couple is being united in the hall
   where the lights are shining brightly.
The people in the hall are listening
   to the notes of "Fuzan," the wedding music.
The newlyweds are in harmony,
   and the family will prosper.

* * *

From Collections of SENRYU, *18th and 19th Centuries*
Translated from the Japanese by R. H. Blyth

SENRYU are colloquial verse, often parodic or satiric, with a form identical to that of haiku—five, seven, five syllables. Senryu, like haiku, imply an echoing of meaning before and after the verse itself. There are about a hundred and twenty thousand Old Senryu, published in numerous collections after 1765. A few which pertain to weddings and new marriage are translated here.

   Did I see her,
     Or did I not?
   The bride hides herself.

* * *

SENRYU

> For some time,
>   The new bride wants
> To run into the house.

* * *

In the Japanese marriage ceremony, two children—the "male butterfly" and the "female butterfly"—pour the wine from a wine vessel, and for this reason the saké is called "butterfly wine." The bride tastes the wine daintily, as if she were a butterfly:

> The bride
>   Sips about a dewdrop
> Of the butterfly wine.

* * *

> The first night
>   The elopers
> Stay at the beautiful place.

* * *

In rice-growing areas, there are often disputes about water and irrigation, but newlyweds are indifferent to such mundane matters:

> Being newly-married before all the world,
>   They are unconcerned
> About the quarrels over water.

* * *

The bride's mother is pleased at the prospect of offspring. She need no longer fear that her daughter will be divorced on the ground of being childless:

> When the daughter
>   Tightens the belly-band,
> Her mother feels relieved.

* * *

When the young mother takes the newly born child to her parents' home, they are over-joyed. The baby is a living Buddha, and no present could be better than this:

> The young bride's present
>   To her parents' home,
> A living *Nyorai*.

* * *

The young wife, putting away her husband's clothes, becomes aware of the faint scent of powder or perfume not her own. Traditionally gentle and obedient, the Japanese bride quietly continues her work:

> The bride puts them away,
>   Folding in her breast
> The lingering scent.

* * *

The disillusioned bride is described in a parodic verse:

> The young wife's dreams
>   Wander
> Over the corridor.

PART IV
Twentieth Century

A<small>FTER THE SEVENTEENTH</small> century, wedding poems were no longer composed by the hundreds, but many were written in the eighteenth and nineteenth centuries, and an increasing number after 1900. Part Four of this book consists entirely of twentieth-century poems, in two sections, the first a group of translations and the second a group of poems from England, Ireland, and the United States.

The first section opens with two Russian folk songs and with lyrics by Alexandr Blok and Boris Pasternak. Following these are poems by Einar Skjæraasen from Norway and by Edith Södergran and P. Mustapää from Finland. The German poet-clergyman Kurt Marti comments ironically upon the hypocrisy of a fashionable church wedding, where "the gentlemen in prosperous tail-coats look discreetly at their watches." Ramón López Velarde's "The Ascension and the Assumption" is reminiscent of the medieval mystical poem. And Samuel Beckett's translation of Salvador Díaz Miron's "Nox" bewails impending disaster, with its refrain:

*Your marriage-feast
will be to-morrow.*

Twentieth-century English poets speak in many different voices, and they echo many different traditions. One recurring motif is the union of Heaven and Earth. In the first century after Christ, the motif appeared in Statius' poem, with Venus, goddess of Love, declaring:

*The sky itself melts at my will
And weds with earth
And clouds break into showers.
So it is that in this world
All things beget their kind,
And thus is life renewed.*

Part IV: Twentieth Century

In the sixteenth century, the critic Scaliger advised poets to tell how the nuptials of Heaven and Earth were celebrated at the beginning of the world, and how by this union all living things were brought forth. He advised poets to tell how these living things, imitating Heaven and Earth, propagated themselves by generation, to the end that immortality, which is denied by the nature of matter, may be attained by the ordered succession of forms. Something of this poetic tradition echoes in the twentieth-century poem by Gray Burr, "What We Listened For in Music." But the same tradition, the union of Heaven and Earth, gives rise to the poem which is perhaps the darkest of the dark poems in this book, C. S. Lewis's "Prelude to Space," in which the poet decries man's attempt to

> *. . . boldly fertilize*
> *The black womb of the unconsenting skies.*

Edith Sitwell also writes bleakly, in a poem titled "Epithalamium," of a time

> *When the vast universal Night shall cover*
> *The earth from Pole to Pole . . .*

But in her "Prothalamium," Miss Sitwell writes more hopefully:

> *Love is all life, the primal law,*
> *The sun and planets to the husbandman,*
> *The kernel and the sap; it is the power*
> *That holds the Golden Rainers in the heavens, bringing us*
> *The calyx of the flower of the world, the spirit*
> *Moving upon the waters, the defeat*
> *Of all time's ravages.*

The last and youngest voice in this book is a hopeful one, speaking in the poem "This and More," written for the wedding of Lane Leidig and Susan Doyle, sophomores at Pasadena City College. Glenn Siebert, friend of the couple and best man at the wedding, composed the poem to be read as part of the ritual at the Oneonta Congregational Church, October 26, 1968. Siebert's poem is a fine example of today's new poetry, created in an old tradition, to bring deeper meaning and personal relevance to the wedding rite.

Translations

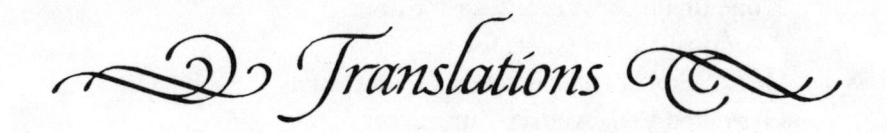

RUSSIAN FOLK SONGS

Translated from the Russian by Michael Daly

As If from Her Nest

As if from her nest,
Her warm little nest,
The young bird has fluttered
Away from the apple-bough,
Away to the open meadowlands,
The green meadowlands, the grassy meadowlands;
There she has pulled up a blade of grass,
Then tossed it aside;
But afterwards she has plucked, the little bird has plucked,
Has plucked a poppy
And fallen in love with it.
And so from under her mother's care,
The fair maiden has come forth,
Come forth, rushed forward,
The sweet fair maiden, Avdótiushka.
Into the wide courtyard
The sweet Avdótiushka has gone,
Into the verdant garden and into the grove of cedars.
The dear little Nikoláievna has sat down
At a new oak table,
And has been watching the guests, newly arrived,
All newly arrived, all strangers to her.

And she has selected a bridegroom.
None of those were pleasing to her.
Avdótiushka has taken for her own,
Dear Nikoláievna has taken for her own,
Has taken you, Andréi, our master,
You, Andréi Polikárpovich.
And having selected, now has fallen in love,
Fallen in love with him, become proud of him.
"Oh, how dear he is to me!
Oh, how dear to my heart is he!
Oh, how I never tire of gazing at him!
Oh, how I can never gaze at him enough!
Oh, how I never want to part from him!"

Mariushka's Wedding Song

Her mother has advised Máriushka,
Advised her dear daughter Efimóvna [1]—
"Do not go, my child,
Do not go, my dear one,
Into your father's orchard for apples;
Or to catch the mottled butterflies,
Or to scare away the little birds;
Do not break in upon the nightingale's song.
For if you pick the apples,
The tree will shrivel,
And if you catch the mottled butterfly,
The butterfly will die;
And if you scare away the little bird,
The bird will never come back;
And if you stop the clear-voiced nightingale,
The nightingale will sing no more:

[1] Patronymic.

Yet snatch, my child,
My dear one, snatch
The shining falcon [2] in the open meadowland,
In the green, open meadowland."

Dear Máriushka has snatched,
Dear Efimóvna has snatched
The shining falcon in the open meadowland,
The green, open meadowland.
She has perched him upon her hand,
She has brought him to her mother.
"My dear mother, Gosudárvinia,
I have caught the shining falcon."

* * *

ALEXANDR BLOK, 1880-1921
Translated from the Russian by Michael Daly

I Planted My Bright Paradise

I planted my bright paradise
And enclosed it round with a high stockade,
And through the blue air, to my wonderful place,
Comes my mother for her dear son.

"My son, my dear, where are you?" —Silence.
The sun grows ripe above my stockade
And now it pours forth its full warmth
Into my valley of paradise.

[2] Bridegroom.

And with such care my mother roams round
My garden-bowers, my legacy,
And she calls anew: "My son! Where are you?"—
So careful not to crush the flowers . . .

All is still. Does she know
That a heart is ripening behind the stockade?
That all former joys are now empty and gone,
Since I have tasted the wine of paradise?

* * *

BORIS PASTERNAK, 1890-1960

Translated from the Russian by Michael Daly

The Wedding (1957)[1]

Across the courtyard
The wedding-guests stroll;
They have come with a concertina
To spend the night at the house of the bride.

Behind the host's doors,
Covered in thick felt,
From one in the morning 'til seven
The chatter is low and subdued.

But at dawn, when you sleep
Such a sleep that could last forever,
The accordion breaks in again,
The sound from the wedding.

[1] One of the poems published with *Doctor Zhivago*

And the musician begins again,
Strewing notes from the accordion all around,
Amid clapping of hands and flashes from necklaces,
In the din of the festivities.

Again, again, and again
Pounds the beat of the *chástushka* [2]
Bursting in to the sleepers in bed
From out of the merry-making.

And one woman, as white as snow,
In the midst of the whistling and clamor,
Strikes out once again in a pea-hen step,
Moving rhythmically from side to side.

Her head keeps time with the beat
As her right hand throbs
All the while to the tune—
Pea-hen, pea-hen, pea-hen.

Then suddenly the gusto and noise of the playing,
The tread of the dancers in a ring,
Suddenly all falls to oblivion,
And sinks, as engulfed by water.

The noisy courtyard awakes;
A commonplace echo of business
Interrupts the conversation
And peals of laughter.

In the boundless sky above,
Flying like the wind are dove-blue patches—
A flock of doves rushing upwards,
Rushing upwards from the dove-cotes.

[2] Form of Russian folk verse.

And to see them makes one feel,
In the trailing-off of the wedding,
Wishes for many years' happiness,
Sent out like doves on the wing.

Life itself is truly just a moment,
Only a dissolving
Of ourselves among all others,
As if we gave ourselves as gifts.

Only a wedding, only the depths of a window
That it breaks through from below;
Only a song, only a dream,
Only a blue dove.

* * *

EINAR SKJÆRAASEN, 1900-
Translated from the Norwegian by Martin Allwood and
Inga Wilhelmsen Allwood

The Word of God

The word of God is she whom you love
She who met you with a smile
And body to body, soul to soul
Gave you to know
That the circuit of longing between man and woman
Was closed.

The word of God is the child you conceived with her
The son who clings to your legs
And calls you father,

And after you is the next step
On the way from age to age.

The word of God is the thought that breaks
Away from your happy safety
To stretch its arms around the world
And live and suffer there
— Yes
To be with all
As if it were your own.

The wrought metals,
The wreaking, plowing, harrowing steel
You use
The grain that runs from your hands,
The field that rises and billows
With golden harvests under the sky
— These are the word of God.

Flowers and insects and stars
And all the things whose names you cannot tell,
Whose laws you do not know,
And all that lives in you
So small that the heart can close around it,
So great that the seas and the mountains are as nothing,
These are the word of God.

The word of God is the white expanse at last
Where the whirl within us shall fall
Like snow in the snow,
Where you yet once more, before the tracks are lost in
    the dark,
Must turn about and *see*
— And render thanks for all that in your heart
Was the word of God.

Part IV: Twentieth Century

The word of God is time after snow-time
When some shall be spellbound
By the twitter of migrant birds in the trees
And growing things in the sunny slopes
And think they remind us of you
— — — For you were a lover in the world.

* * *

EDITH SÖDERGRAN, 1892-1923

Translated from the Finnish by Erik Wahlgren and
Martin S. Allwood

The Land That Is Not

I long for the land that is not,
For all that is, I weary of desiring.
The moon is telling me in silvern runes
Of the land that is not,
The land, where all our wishes are wondrously fulfilled,
The land where all our shackles fall,
The land where our bleeding forehead cools
In the dew of the moon.
My life was a burning illusion.
But one thing I found and one thing I really gained—
The road to the land that is not.

In the land that is not
There walks my beloved with a glittering crown.
Who is my beloved? The night is dark
And the stars quiver in answer.
Who is my beloved? What is his name?

The heavens arch higher and higher
And a human being is drowned in endless mists
And knows no answer.
But a human being is nothing but certainty.
And it stretches its arms higher than all heavens.
And there comes an answer: I am the one you love
                              and always shall love.

* * *

P. MUSTAPÄÄ, 1899-

Translated from the Finnish by Richard Impola

Folk Tale

I am still far away.

I will arrive tomorrow.
Hey, my pack, my laughing pack!
Hey, my friendly walking stick!
Tomorrow we shall arrive.

At a beautiful time.
Just when the old sexton opens the loft of the belfry.
Steam bath, Saturday steam bath.
The music of the round
Sounds in the village.

I am still far away.
A mist, a wild wizard's mist
Seeks the hollows, mounds, shadows,
Groups of aspen trees.

Slippery rocks under foot,
Stumps with staring eyes along the roadside.
Welcome to you,
Welcome, I am a bridegroom,
The bridegroom of happiness.

And so wildly in love.

* * *

KURT MARTI, 1921-

Translated from the German by Christa Wolf and Virginia Tufte

The Unbidden Wedding Guest

The church bells thunder out their roundest tone;
photographers snap pictures, bodies bent.
The organ roars the notes of Mendelssohn,
The clergyman comes in, and with him Christendom.

The ladies kneel, and low-cut gowns reveal
their naked shoulders, piquant, photogenic;
the gentlemen in prosperous tail-coats
look discreetly at their watches.

Softly as in a movie whirs the liturgy,
marking time for feast of opulence.
A lone voice whispers, "Blasphemy!"
The Lord. But Him they fail to hear.

RAMÓN LÓPEZ VELARDE, 1888-1921
Translated from the Spanish by H. R. Hays

The Ascension and the Assumption

There lives beside me here an unknown woman,
Invisible and perfect, who exalts me
With every sunset and with every dawn.

Above all caricatures and parodies,
My body with her own enlaced,
We rise to heaven like two hosts ...

Reciprocal dogma of the heart:
Through its own virtue and through another's virtue
Ascension and Assumption both in one!

Her heart, theology and mist,
Buttoned to the redness of my heart,
Translates into starry music
The sacrament of the Eucharist.

The fantasm of plaster flies incognito,
And when we emerge from the atmosphere's end
She gives me half her profile with her dialogue,
A quarter with her kiss.

God, who sees that I, without a woman,
Accomplish nothing either great or small,
Gave me, as guardian angel, a feminine angel.

Lord, I am thankful for this mighty gift
By which the fall is turned into a flight,

Part IV: Twentieth Century

A marriage in the midst of life's misfortunes,
Ascension and Assumption both in one!

* * *

SALVADOR DÍAZ MIRON, 1859-1928
Translated from the Spanish by Samuel Beckett

Nox

THIS TWENTIETH-CENTURY Mexican poem falls into the category of dark or "anti-"nuptial poems, which usually portend revenge, murder, or other disaster.

> No syrup or perfume
> is like your prattle....
> What spiced and sugared
> lozenge in
> your mouth will melt
> its honey and amber
> when oh virgin alone
> with me you speak?
>
> Your marriage-feast
> will be to-morrow.
>
> To the glory of night
> you turn your face,
> fairer than the roses
> at the window;
> and your golden tresses
> stream on the breeze
> and your troubled face
> chances to move me....

Your marriage-feast
will be to-morrow.

On a cabal a comet
pounces in the gloom.
It is a weeping emblem,
a sign of song.
Point and stroke
compose the star;
it figures a note,
depicts a tear.

Your marriage-feast
will be to-morrow.

Invisible flock,
the cranes pass over,
beating high
their mighty wings;
dismal, harsh,
they cry and rail,
as if bewailing
a disaster.

Your marriage-feast
will be to-morrow.

A hovering cloudlet,
rising, falling,
languid, flaccid,
solemn, white,
feigns in doubly
symbolic aspect
the bridal veil,
the winding-sheet.

Part IV: Twentieth Century

Your marriage-feast
will be to-morrow.

By the gauze that takes
on magic form,
Scorpio queries,
while his alpha
is budding crimson,
bleeding portent. . . .
And love and grief
whet separate arms!

Your marriage-feast
will be to-morrow.

Ah! would the vile earth
that through the vast
abysses wheels
its slavish track
might end its rounds
and be dispelled,
dissolved in wisps
of tenuous rack.

Your marriage-feast
will be to-morrow.

The sea's faint wave
stirs on the shore,
flooding, drowning
nor peoples nor aught.
Of Sodom's fire
I see no ember,
and the red arrow
of lightning is quivered.

SALVADOR DÍAZ MIRON

Your marriage-feast
will be to-morrow.

Ah Tirsa! already
the hour and my heart
misgives and my soul
in a lark's trill is flown.
Dawn unfolds
her nacreous veil
and Lucifer raises
his pale pearl.

English

A.E. HOUSMAN, 1859-1936

Epithalamium

He is here, Urania's son,
Hymen come from Helicon;
God that glads the lover's heart,
He is here to join and part.
So the groomsman quits your side
And the bridegroom seeks the bride:
Friend and comrade yield you o'er
To her that hardly loves you more.

Now the sun his skyward beam
Has tilted from the Ocean stream.
Light the Indies, laggard sun:
Happy bridegroom, day is done,
And the star from Oeta's steep
Calls to bed but not to sleep.

Happy bridegroom Hesper brings
All desired and timely things.
All whom morning sends to roam,
Hesper loves to lead them home.
Home return who him behold,
Child to mother, sheep to fold,
Bird to nest from wandering wide:
Happy bridegroom, seek your bride.

Pour it out, the golden cup
Given and guarded, brimming up,
Safe through jostling markets borne
And the thicket of the thorn;
Folly spurned and danger past,
Pour it to the god at last.

Now, to smother noise and light,
Is stolen abroad the wildering night,
And the blotting shades confuse
Path and meadow full of dews;
And the high heavens, that all control,
Turn in silence round the pole.
Catch the starry beams they shed
Prospering the marriage bed,
And breed the land that reared your prime
Sons to stay the rot of time.
All is quiet, no alarms;
Nothing fear of nightly harms.
Safe you sleep on guarded ground,
And in silent circle round
The thoughts of friends keep watch and ward,
Harnessed angels, hand on sword.

* * *

GERTRUDE STEIN, 1874-1946

Prothalamium for Bobolink and His Louisa A Poem

GERTRUDE STEIN wrote her "Prothalamium" in 1939 to celebrate the engagement of a young California student, Robert Bartlett Haas, to

Part IV: Twentieth Century

Louise Antoinette Krause. Miss Stein had never met the couple, but she and Haas had become fast friends through several years of correspondence. The poem is of special interest because Gertrude Stein, usually the most unconventional of authors, here draws heavily on conventional motifs of the classical epithalamium, compressing them into a unique shorthand for twentieth-century readers, and the poem yields its meaning only when read in the light of conventions that have functioned in European literature for thirty centuries or more.

The very first line is baffling unless the reader recognizes it as an exhortation. The poet is urging the couple to make love without restraint, to "love like anything," the kind of exhortation that appears in epithalamia from the time of Sappho. Miss Stein, like the classical nuptial poet, is assuming the role of *choragus*, or master of ceremonies, whose primary function is to urge the couple to unite, but who also directs the celebration, provides a running commentary on the nuptial events, and philosophizes on marriage as an institution. Many writers of nuptial poetry comment on the relationship of the marital union to the current state of the world, and Miss Stein views this particular marriage in the context of a "war-time" world which yet has some hope of attaining peace.

After enjoining the couple to consummate the union, the poet introduces several contrasts and paradoxes conventional in nuptial poetry—war and peace, day and night, and two in one. She builds the war and peace motif into a refrain, blending it with other motifs in the crescendo of the second stanza and culminating with "Peace-time" after the union of the couple. In the third stanza, we see an exchange of commonplaces between two choruses of wedding guests: "They say . . . And we say . . . And they say . . ." In the closing lines of the poem, the poet-master of ceremonies takes a bow ("Thank you") and makes formal announcement of the engagement.

> Love like anything
> In war-time
> Day and night
> In peace and war-time
> Birds are Bobolinks
> In war-time
> Girls are Louises
> In war time

War time Peace time. Two in one. In Peace-time.
Two in one and one in two. In War-time. Louise
and Bobolink are one. In Peace-time in War-time
                Peace-time

    They say
    How do you do. And we say
    How do you do too.
    And they say very well I thank you
    Which pleases them
    And us too
    Two and two that is one is two
    which is you
    Louise and Bobolink.

    Thank you.
    They are engaged. To be married.

            *   *   *

JOHN MASEFIELD, 1878-1967

From Souvenir Programme, The Wedding of Her Royal Highness

Prayer for the Royal Marriage

Princess Elizabeth and Lieutenant Philip Mountbatten, R. N.
Westminster Abbey, 20th November, 1947

    What is the Crown, but something set above
    The jangle and the jargon and the hate
    Of strivers after power in the State,
    A symbol, like a banner, for men's love?

    When hope is dim and luck is out of joint,
    When enemies within, without, assail,
    Where a Crown shines, the courage cannot fail,
    There a land's spirit finds a rallying-point.

Part IV: Twentieth Century

> To those young lands, the countries of our kin,
> The friends in need, the comrades in despair,
> Our allies steadfast when no others were ...
> But how can Britain praise them? How begin?
>
> To those dear lands, still calling Britain "Home,"
> The Crown is still the link with Britain's past,
> The consecrated thing that must outlast
> Folly and hate and other human foam.
>
> To those, as to ourselves, this marriage time
> Summons all hearts from their accustomed ways
> To pray that hidden strengths, supreme, sublime,
> May from their glory bless this couple's days.
>
> To pray, that She, our Future Queen, may hear
> Through many happy years, the bells rejoice,
> Telling of People glad, a Sovereign dear,
> A Land restored, a Purpose again clear,
> With wind-delighting clamour of glad voice.

* * *

JAMES JOYCE, 1882-1941

From *Chamber Music*

1

> Strings in the earth and air
>   Make music sweet;
> Strings by the river where
>   The willows meet.

There's music along the river
   For Love wanders there,
Pale flowers on his mantle,
   Dark leaves on his hair.

All softly playing,
   With head to the music bent,
And fingers straying
   Upon an instrument.

II

The twilight turns from amethyst
   To deep and deeper blue,
The lamp fills with a pale green glow
   The trees of the avenue.

The old piano plays an air,
   Sedate and slow and gay;
She bends upon the yellow keys,
   Her head inclines this way.

Shy thoughts and grave wide eyes and hands
   That wander as they list—
The twilight turns to darker blue
   With lights of amethyst.

III

At that hour when all things have repose,
   O lonely watcher of the skies,
   Do you hear the night wind and the sighs
Of harps playing unto Love to unclose
   The pale gates of sunrise?

When all things repose do you alone
   Awake to hear the sweet harps play
   To Love before him on his way,
And the night wind answering in antiphon
   Till night is overgone?

Play on, invisible harps, unto Love,
   Whose way in heaven is aglow
   At that hour when soft lights come and go,
Soft sweet music in the air above
   And in the earth below.

IV

When the shy star goes forth in heaven
   All maidenly, disconsolate,
Hear you amid the drowsy even
   One who is singing by your gate.
His song is softer than the dew
   And he is come to visit you.

O bend no more in revery
   When he at eventide is calling,
Nor muse: Who may this singer be
   Whose song about my heart is falling?
Know you by this, the lover's chant,
   'Tis I that am your visitant.

V

Lean out of the window,
   Goldenhair,
I heard you singing
   A merry air.

My book was closed;
   I read no more,
Watching the fire dance
   On the floor.

I have left my book,
   I have left my room,
For I heard you singing
   Through the gloom.

Singing and singing
   A merry air,
Lean out of the window,
   Goldenhair.

VI

I would in that sweet bosom be
   (O sweet it is and fair it is!)
Where no rude wind might visit me.
   Because of sad austerities
I would in that sweet bosom be.

I would be ever in that heart
   (O soft I knock and soft entreat her!)
Where only peace might be my part.
   Austerities were all the sweeter
So I were ever in that heart.

VII

My love is in a light attire
   Among the apple-trees,
Where the gay winds do most desire
   To run in companies.

Part IV: Twentieth Century

There, where the gay winds stay to woo
   The young leaves as they pass,
My love goes slowly, bending to
   Her shadow on the grass;

And where the sky's a pale blue cup
   Over the laughing land,
My love goes lightly, holding up
   Her dress with dainty hand.

VIII

Who goes amid the green wood
   With springtide all adorning her?
Who goes amid the merry green wood
   To make it merrier?

Who passes in the sunlight
   By ways that know the light footfall?
Who passes in the sweet sunlight
   With mien so virginal?

The ways of all the woodland
   Gleam with a soft and golden fire—
For whom does all the sunny woodland
   Carry so brave attire?

O, it is for my true love
   The woods their rich apparel wear—
O, it is for my own true love,
   That is so young and fair.

IX

Winds of May, that dance on the sea,
Dancing a ring-around in glee

From furrow to furrow, while overhead
The foam flies up to be garlanded,
In silvery arches spanning the air,
Saw you my true love anywhere?
    Welladay! Welladay!
    For the winds of May!
Love is unhappy when love is away!

X

Bright cap and streamers,
    He sings in the hollow:
    Come follow, come follow,
      All you that love.
Leave dreams to the dreamers
    That will not after,
    That song and laughter
      Do nothing move.

With ribbons streaming
    He sings the bolder;
    In troop at his shoulder
      The wild bees hum.
And the time of dreaming
    Dreams is over—
    As lover to lover,
      Sweetheart, I come.

XI

Bid adieu, adieu, adieu,
    Bid adieu to girlish days,
Happy Love is come to woo
    Thee and woo thy girlish ways—
The zone that doth become thee fair,
The snood upon thy yellow hair.

Part IV: Twentieth Century

When thou hast heard his name upon
   The bugles of the cherubim
Begin thou softly to unzone
   Thy girlish bosom unto him
And softly to undo the snood
That is the sign of maidenhood.

XII

What counsel has the hooded moon
   Put in thy heart, my shyly sweet,
Of Love in ancient plenilune,
   Glory and stars beneath his feet—
A sage that is but kith and kin
With the comedian Capuchin?

Believe me rather that am wise
   In disregard of the divine,
A glory kindles in those eyes,
   Trembles to starlight. Mine, O Mine!
No more be tears in moon or mist
For thee, sweet sentimentalist.

XIII

Go seek her out all courteously,
   And say I come,
Wind of spices whose song is ever
   Epithalamium.
O, hurry over the dark lands
   And run upon the sea
For seas and land shall not divide us
   My love and me.

Now, wind, of your good courtesy
   I pray you go,
And come into her little garden
   And sing at her window;
Singing: The bridal wind is blowing
   For Love is at his noon;
And soon will your true love be with you,
   Soon, O soon.

XIV

My dove, my beautiful one,
   Arise, arise!
   The night-dew lies
Upon my lips and eyes.

The odorous winds are weaving
   A music of sighs:
   Arise, arise,
My dove, my beautiful one!

I wait by the cedar tree,
   My sister, my love.
   White breast of the dove,
My breast shall be your bed.

The pale dew lies
   Like a veil on my head.
   My fair one, my fair dove,
Arise, arise!

XV

From dewy dreams, my soul, arise,
   From love's deep slumber and from death,

Part IV: Twentieth Century

For lo! the trees are full of sighs
   Whose leaves the morn admonisheth.

Eastward the gradual dawn prevails
   Where softly-burning fires appear,
Making to tremble all those veils
   Of grey and golden gossamer.

While sweetly, gently, secretly,
   The flowery bells of morn are stirred
And the wise choirs of faery
   Begin (innumerous!) to be heard.

XVI

O cool is the valley now
   And there, love, will we go
For many a choir is singing now
   Where Love did sometime go.
And hear you not the thrushes calling,
   Calling us away?
O cool and pleasant is the valley
   And there, love, will we stay.

* * *

EZRA POUND, 1885-

Dance Figure
For the Marriage in Cana of Galilee

Dark eyed,
O woman of my dreams,

Ivory sandaled,
There is none like thee among the dancers,
None with swift feet.

I have not found thee in the tents,
In the broken darkness.
I have not found thee at the well-head
Among the women with pitchers.

Thine arms are as a young sapling under the bark;
Thy face as a river with lights.

White as an almond are thy shoulders;
As new almonds stripped from the husk.
They guard thee not with eunuchs;
Not with bars of copper.

Gilt turquoise and silver are in the place of thy rest.
A brown robe, with threads of gold woven in patterns,
    hast thou gathered about thee,
O Nathat-Ilkanaie, "Tree-at-the-river."

As a rillet among the sedge are thy hands upon me;
Thy fingers a frosted stream.

Thy maidens are white like pebbles;
Their music about thee!

There is none like thee among the dancers;
None with swift feet.

* * *

Part IV: Twentieth Century

EDITH SITWELL, 1887-1964

Prothalamium

For the Marriage of the Duke and Duchess of Kent, 8th June 1961

Now the great flower of the world
And its gold bee, the sun
With all its hives and lives of honeyed light
—The Queens and lilies born on British soil—
The Queens with eyelids like the young narcissus
Shall bless this youth and innocence—young people
Like the spring rainbows, risen from all growth,
The sap and singing, tall among the trees.

The music of the air, the flame of flowers
Are lustrous with their youth, like the first spring when
    it began
In the young world before the Fall of Man.

The white bride and the forest of white flowers
Upon the Altar, and white lightnings of the dew
(Each drop Altair and Sirius) fallen from the petals
Seem one. And like the music of the air,
The young children following—
The bridesmaids with their curls as blond as water.

          Love is all life, the primal law,
The sun and planets to the husbandman,
The kernel and the sap; it is the power
That holds the Golden Rainers in the heavens, bringing us
The calyx of the flower of the world, the spirit
Moving upon the waters, the defeat
Of all time's ravages.

Upon this happy day—
Even for the old, whose winter was flowerless, whose
    bones are sunless
(Yet older than Spring), their winter breaks again in flower
Till summer grows from a long-shadowed kiss.

Who was it cried, "This is no time for sowing or begetting.
The East is yellow with fear, and the West is red with its
    setting"?

Although a gray bough drips
With dews of death, still the lost floras of the world
Lie on young cheeks, young lips.

Epithalamium

When the vast universal Night shall cover
The earth from Pole to Pole, and like a lover
Invade your heart, that was at once my stone,
And I your Sisyphus, in one abyss
We two shall lie in an eternal kiss
So, breast on breast, heart close to heart, we lie
As those within the grave's eternity,
And dream our arms hold the horizons deep
Where the strong suns come freshened from deep seas,
The continents beyond discoveries,
Immortal youth, and the god's wisdom—sleep.
How should I dream that I must wake alone
With a void coffin of sad flesh and bone:
You, with the small immortal Serpent's kiss,
You, the dull rumor of the dust's renown—
The Polar night, a boulder rolling down
My heart, your Sisyphus, to your abyss
Where is nor light, nor dark, nor soul nor heart to eat;
Only the falling dust of all the dead,
                      the sound of passing feet.

Part IV: Twentieth Century

E. E. CUMMINGS, 1894-1962

this little bride & groom are

this little bride & groom are
standing) in a kind
of crown he dressed
in black candy she

veiled with candy white
carrying a bouquet of
pretend flowers this
candy crown with this candy

little bride & little
groom in it kind of stands on
a thin ring which stands on a much
less thin very much more

big & kinder of ring & which
kinder of stands on a
much more than very much
biggest & thickest & kindest

of ring & all one two three rings
are cake & everything is protected by
cellophane against anything(because
nothing really exists

* * *

ROBERT GRAVES, 1895-

At the Savoy Chapel

[From *World's Press News*, 22 February, 1945. "Alexander Clifford, the war correspondent, is today marrying Flight Officer Jenny Nicholson, daughter of Robert Graves. They met in the front line."]

Up to the wedding, formal with heirloom lace,
Press-cameras, carnations out of season,
Well-mellowed priest and well-trained choristers,

The relatives come marching, such as meet
Only at weddings and at funerals,
The elder generation with the eldest.

Family features for years undecided
What look to wear against a loveless world
Fix, as the wind veers, in the same grimace.

Each eyes the others with a furtive pity:
"Heavens, how she has aged—and he,
Grey hair and sunken cheeks, what a changed man!"

They stare wistfully at the bride (released
From brass buttons and the absurd salute)
In long white gown, bouquet and woman's pride.

"How suitable!" they whisper, and the whisper
"How suitable!" rustles from pew to pew;
To which I nod suitably grave assent.

Now for you, loving ones, who kneel at the altar
And preside afterwards at table—
The trophy sword that shears the cake recalling

Part IV: Twentieth Century

What god you entertained last year together,
His bull neck looped with guts,
Trampling corpse-carpet through the villages—

Here is my private blessing: so to remain
As today you are, with features
Resolute and unchangeably your own.

The Wedding

When down I went to the rust-red quarry
I was informed, by birds, of your resolve
To live with me for ever and a day—
The day being always new and antecedent.
What could we ask of Nature? Nothing more
Than to outdo herself in our behalf.

Blossoms of caper, though they smell sweet,
Have never sailed the air like butterflies
Circling in innocent dance around each other
Over the cliff and out across the bay;
Nor has broom-blossom scorched a man's finger
With golden fire, kindled by sun.

Come, maids of honour and pages chosen
To attend this wedding, charged to perform
Incomparable feats—dance, caper-blossom!
Scorch, blossom of broom, our married fingers—
Though crowds of almost-men and almost-women
Howl for their lost immediacy.

* * *

C. S. LEWIS, 1898-1963

Prelude to Space
An Epithalamium

THE DARK or "anti-"nuptial poem has for centuries been used for social commentary. In this poem C. S. Lewis ironically dramatizes a union between Heaven and Earth.

> So Man, grown vigorous now,
> Holds himself ripe to breed,
> Daily devises how
> To ejaculate his seed
> And boldly fertilize
> The black womb of the unconsenting skies.
>
> Some now alive expect
> (I am told) to see the large,
> Steel member grow erect,
> Turgid with the fierce charge
> Of our whole planet's skill,
> Courage, wealth, knowledge, concentrated will;
>
> Straining with lust to stamp
> Our likeness on the abyss—
> Bombs, gallows, Belsen camp,
> Pox, polio, Thais' kiss
> Or Judas', Moloch's fires
> And Torquemada's (sons resemble sires).
>
> Shall we, when the grim shape
> Roars upward, dance and sing?

Yes: if we honour rape,
If we take pride to fling
So bountifully on space
The sperm of our long woes, our large disgrace.

The Small Man Orders His Wedding

With tambourines of amber, queens
In rose and lily garlanded
Shall go beside my noble bride
With dance and din and harmony,
And sabre clash and tabor crash
And lantern-light and torches flash
On shield and helmet, plume and sash,
The flower of all my armoury;

Till drawn at length by tawny strength
Of lions, lo! her chariot;
Their pride will brook no bridle—look,
No bit they bear, no farrier
Ere shod those feet that plod the street
Silent as ghosts; their savage heat
Is gentled as they draw my sweet,
New tamed herself, to marry me.

New swell from all the belfries tall,
Till towers reel, the revelry
Of iron tongue untiring swung
To booms and clangs of merriment!
While some prepare with trumpet blare
Before my gates to greet us there
When home we come; and everywhere
Let drum be rumbled steadily.

Once in, the roar and din no more
Are heard. The hot festivity
And blazing dies; from gazing eyes
These shadowy halls deliver her.
Yet neither flute nor blither lute
With pluck of amorous string be mute
Where happy maids their queen salute
And candle flames are quivering.

With decent stealth o'er fleecy wealth
Of carpets tripping soberly,
Depart each maid! Your part is played
And I to all her nobleness
Must mate my bare estate. How fair
The whole room has become! The air
Burns as with incense everywhere
Around, beneath, and over her.

What flame before our chamber door
Shines in on love's security?
Fiercer than day, its piercing ray
Pours round us unendurably.
It's Aphrodite's saffron light,
And Jove's monarchal presence bright
And Genius burning through the night
The torch of man's futurity.

For her the swords of furthest lords
Have flashed in fields ethereal;
The dynasts seven incline from heaven
With glad regard and serious,
And ponder there beyond our air
The infinite unborn, and care
For history, while the mortal pair
Lie drowned in dreaming weariness.

Part IV: Twentieth Century

YVOR WINTERS, 1900-1968

The Marriage

Incarnate for our marriage you appeared,
Flesh living in the spirit and endeared
By minor graces and slow sensual change.
Through every nerve we made our spirits range.
We fed our minds on every mortal thing:
The lacy fronds of carrots in the spring,
Their flesh sweet on the tongue, the salty wine
From bitter grapes, which gathered through the vine
The mineral drouth of autumn concentrate,
Wild spring in dream escaping, the debate
Of flesh and spirit on those vernal nights,
Its resolution in naïve delights,
The young kids bleating softly in the rain—
All this to pass, not to return again.
And when I found your flesh did not resist,
It was the living spirit that I kissed,
It was the spirit's change in which I lay:
Thus, mind in mind we waited for the day.
When flesh shall fall away, and, falling, stand
Wrinkling with shadow over face and hand,
Still I shall meet you on the verge of dust
And know you as a faithful vestige must.
And, in commemoration of our lust,
May our heirs seal us in a single urn,
A single spirit never to return.

W. H. AUDEN, 1907-

Epithalamion
For Giuseppe Antonio Borgese and Elisabeth Mann (Nov. 23, 1939)

While explosives blow to dust
Friends and hopes, we cannot pray,
Absolute conviction must
Seem the whole of life to youth,
Battle's stupid gross event
Keep all learning occupied:
Yet the seed becomes the tree;
Happier savants may decide
That this quiet wedding of
A Borgese and a Mann
Planted human unity;
Hostile kingdoms of the truth,
Fighting fragments of content,
Here were reconciled by love,
Modern policy begun
    On this day.

A priori dogmas brought
Into one collective will
All the European thought:
Eagle theologians swept
With an autocratic eye
Hungry for potential foes
The whole territory of truth
Where the great cathedrals rose;
Gentle to instinctive crimes,
With a sharp indulgence heard
Paradox-debating youth,
Listened where the injured wept

Part IV: Twentieth Century

For the first rebellious sigh,
And unerringly at times
On some small progressive bird
    Swooped to kill.

But beneath them as they flew
Merchants with more prudent gaze
Broke eternity in two:
Unconcerned at the controls
Sat an ascetic engineer
In whose intellectual hand
Worlds of dull material lay,
All that bankers understand;
While elected by the heart
Out of sentiment, a lamb
With haemorrhages night and day
Saved enthusiastic souls;
Sorrow apt to interfere,
Wit that spoils romantic art,
In the social diagram
    Knew their place.

Yet no lie has only friends
Too polite to ask for proof:
Patriots, peering through the lens
Of their special discipline
At the map of knowledge, see
Superstition overcome
As all national frontiers melt
In a true imperium;
Fearing foreign skills no more,
Feel in each conative act
Such a joy as Dante felt
When, a total failure in
An inferior city, he,
Dreaming out his anger, saw

W. H. AUDEN

All the scattered leaves of fact
   Bound by love.

May this bed of marriage be
Symbol now of the rebirth
Asked of old humanity:
Let creative limbs explore
All creation's pleasure then;
Laughing horses, rocks that scream,
All the flowers that ever flew
Through the banquet of a dream,
Find in you a common love
Of extravagant sanity;
Till like Leonardo who,
Jostled by the sights of war
And unpleasant greedy men,
At Urbino watched a dove,
Your experience justify
   Life on earth.

Grateful in your happiness,
Let your Ariels fly away
To a gay unconsciousness
And a freely-chosen task:
Shame at our shortcomings makes
Lame magicians of us all,
Forcing our invention to
An illegal miracle
And a theatre of disguise;
Brilliantly your angels took
Every lover's role for you,
Wore seduction like a mask
Or were frigid for your sakes;
Set these shadows, now your eyes
On the whole of substance look,
   Free to-day.

(277)

Kindly to each other turn,
Every timid vice forgive
With a quaker's quiet concern
For the uncoercive law,
Till your double wish be one,
Till, as you successful lie,
Begotten possibility,
Censoring the nostalgic sigh
To be nothing or be right,
Form its ethical resolve
Now to suffer and to be:
Though the kingdoms are at war,
All the peoples see the sun,
All the dwellings stand in light,
All the unconquered worlds revolve,
    Life must live.

Vowing to redeem the State,
Now let every girl and boy
To the heaven of the Great
All their prayers and praises lift:
Mozart with ironic breath
Turning poverty to song,
Goethe innocent of sin
Placing every human wrong,
Blake the industrious visionary,
Tolstoi the great animal,
Hellas-loving Hoelderlin,
Wagner who obeyed his gift
Organised his wish for death
Into a tremendous cry,
Looking down upon us, all
    Wish us joy.

DYLAN THOMAS, 1914-1953

On the Marriage of a Virgin

Walking alone in a multitude of loves when morning's light
Surprised in the opening of her nightlong eyes
His golden yesterday asleep upon the iris
And this day's sun leapt up the sky out of her thighs
Was miraculous virginity old as loaves and fishes,
Though the moment of a miracle is unending lightning
And the shipyards of Galilee's footprints hide a navy of
   doves.

No longer will the vibrations of the sun desire on
Her deepsea pillow where once she married alone,
Her heart all ears and eyes, lips catching the avalanche
Of the golden ghost who ringed with his streams her
   mercury bone,
Who under the lids of her windows hoisted his golden
   luggage,
For a man sleeps where fire leapt down and she learns
   through his arm
That other sun, the jealous coursing of the unrivalled blood.

* * *

MAY SARTON, 1912-

Prothalamium

How pure the hearts of lovers as they walk
Through the rich quiet fields
Where the stiff wheat grows heavy on the stalk

Part IV: Twentieth Century

And over barley and its paler golds,
The air is bright—

Would touch it all, embrace, learn it by hand,
Plunging their faces into the thick grain,
To stroke as well as see the cow's soft flank,
To feel the beech trunk harsh under the palm,
And oh, to drink the light!

They do not even walk yet hand in hand,
But every sense is pricked alive so sharp
That life breathes through them from the burning land,
And they could use the wind itself for harp
And pluck the vibrant green.

At first the whole world opens into sense:
They learn their love by looking at the wheat,
And there let fall all that was shy and tense
To walk the season slowly on propitious feet
And be all they have seen.

Now all around them earth moves toward an end,
The gold turning to bronze, the barley tasseled,
The fruit stored up, and soon the sheaves will bend
Their heads together in the rich wedding-bed
All are about to enter.

The hearts of lovers as they walk, how pure;
How cool the wind upon the open palm
As they move on toward harvest, and so sure,
Even this ripening has a marvelous calm.
And a still center.

GRAY BURR, 1919-

What We Listened for in Music

We heard the phoebe calling in the wood
Two notes as pure and clear as abstract love.
Platonic call, I thought, speak to us of
The far, the true, the beautiful, the good.

Again two notes, these more pellucid still,
As though some angelus of heaven rang
Against our earthen sense, and, ghostly, sang
Of all that our corruption could not will.

We stood a moment there, rapt, yet appalled
Until an answer came: two notes as rich,
As absolute, but on a deeper pitch.
Then we knew that earth to earth had called.

* * *

PHILIP LARKIN, 1922-

Wedding Wind

The wind blew all my wedding-day,
And my wedding-night was the night of the high wind;
And a stable door was banging, again and again,
That he must go and shut it, leaving me
Stupid in candlelight, hearing rain,

Part IV: Twentieth Century

Seeing my face in the twisted candlestick,
Yet seeing nothing. When he came back
He said the horses were restless, and I was sad
That any man or beast that night should lack
The happiness I had.

    Now in the day
All's ravelled under the sun by the wind's blowing.
He has gone to look at the floods, and I
Carry a chipped pail to the chicken-run,
Set it down, and stare. All is the wind
Hunting through clouds and forests, thrashing
My apron and the hanging cloths on the line.
Can it be borne, this bodying-forth by wind
Of joy my actions turn on, like a thread
Carrying beads? Shall I be let to sleep
Now this perpetual morning shares my bed?
Can even death dry up
These new delighted lakes, conclude
Our kneeling as cattle by all-generous waters?

    *   *   *

RUTH WHITMAN, 1923-

Cutting the Jewish Bride's Hair

 A twentieth-century American poet here refers to an ancient custom in eastern Europe: the Jewish bride shaved her head, to signify modesty, or submission, or to make her beauty less distracting to her husband. She then wore a marriage wig.

It's to possess more than the skin
that those old world Jews
exacted the hair of their brides.
    Good husband, lover of the Torah,
    does the calligraphy of your bride's hair
    interrupt your page?

Before the clownish friction of flesh
creating out of nothing
a mockup of its begetters,
a miraculous puppet of God,
you must first divorce her from her vanity.

She will snip off her pride,
cut back her appetite to be devoured,
she will keep herself well braided,
her love's furniture will not endanger you,
    but this little amputation
    will shift the balance of the universe.

* * *

VASSAR MILLER, 1924-

Song for a Marriage

Housed in each other's arms,
Thatched with each other's grace,
Your bodies, flint on steel
Striking out fire to fend
The cold away awhile;
With sweat for mortar, brace

Part IV: Twentieth Century

Your walls against the sleet
And the rib-riddling wind.

A house, you house yourselves,
Housed, you will house another,
Scaled to a subtler blueprint
Than architects can draw—
A triple function yours
In this world's winter weather,
Oh, breathing brick and stone,
I look on you with awe.

A fig for praise that calls
Flesh a bundle of sticks,
Kindling for flame that feels
Like swallowing the sun!
Yet luxury turned labor's
No old maid's rancid mix,
But how bone-masonry
Outweighs the skeleton.

* * *

ANN STANFORD, 1925-

Ceremonies

January-June, 1968

I am inside the box
I am there in the dark
And I say to my friends—See
I am saying goodbye

Do not be angry
They do not hear me

The sun is shining
I am the bride
Look, I am being kissed
Jesu, the wedding night

I am too sleepy for love
I am lost in the stained glass
Climbing
I am a gray frog
Out there in the chorus.

* * *

JAMES MERRILL, 1926-

Upon a Second Marriage

   Orchards, we linger here because
Women we love stand propped in your green prisons,
Obedient to such justly bending laws
     Each one longs to take root,
    Lives to confess whatever season's
Pride of blossom or endeavor's fruit
    May to her rustling boughs have risen.

   But autumn reddens the whole mind.
No more, each swears, the dazzle of a year
Shall woo her from your bare cage of loud wind,
     Promise the ring and run
    To burn the altar, reappear

With apple blossoms for the credulous one.
   Orchards, we wonder that we linger here!

   Orchards we planted, trees we shook
To learn what you were bearing, say we stayed
Because one winter twilight we mistook
     Frost on a bleakened bough
   For buds of green, and were afraid
To miss the old persuasion, should we go.
   And the spring came, and discourse made

   Enough of weddings to us all
That, loving her for whom the whole world grows
Fragrant and white, we linger to recall
     As down aisles of cut trees
   How a tall trunk's cross-section shows
Concentric rings, those many marriages
   That life on each live thing bestows.

       *   *   *

ANNE CLUYSENAAR, 1936-

Epithalamium

   The rings of the sun rise
   In cloud above them. A quiver
   Of wind on the pane becomes

   The quiver in his arms of her
   Sleeping form. And through these
   Echoes extends love's power.

Wings open and shut, the sun
Thick in their fans. They flash
On his thought her body's turn.

Dawn has melted their flesh
To a fan of shadows, thrown
The spread fan beyond reach.

Now, in their double darkness,
Shutting. Sleep, then, sleep.
The rings of the sun's expanse

Rest in her body. Timeless,
Your love. It circles a deep
Night, without fear of darkness.

Traced in the rise and fall
Of wings, day, at your window,
Eddies without noise. Able

To hold her body now so
Still, remember the ceremonial
Opaque berries of mistletoe,

Shining from between flights of
Dark leaves, as you shine
From between the shadows of

Her limbs, the year's crown:
Such loving moments have,
Between dark ones, grown.

Not without wisdom, the tide
Of day was met with praise
Of time wasted with pride

Part IV: Twentieth Century

If, without fear, without tears,
You should see again at her side
The rings of a winter sunrise.

* * *

GLENN SIEBERT, 1948-

This and More

Attenders to this day:
Look, the wedding is a reason
To inspect your thoughts; say
Smily wishes to the young wedded,
But see to your own new season—
No trite impediments, no bored white
Winter of cold thoughts imbedded
In mountain crevices of self-pity.
Be gathered into the light,
Into no mere festivity—
But more, a snowballing of hope.
Then you still live; we all
Live on tomorrow when two breaths elope,
Tonight when pulse on pulse sustains
Two lives, these and their sweet flesh . . .
Inhale brisk flowers, then let befall
Whatever dark rains
Come; you see lives mesh
Today, today you bystand bliss.
Attend all this.